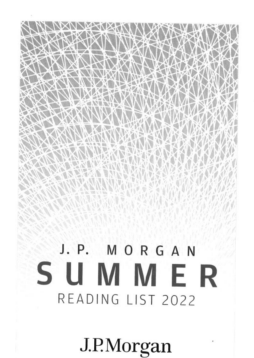

J.P. MORGAN
SUMMER
READING LIST 2022

J.P.Morgan

THE COMPREHENSIVE GUIDE

NFTs
DIGITAL ARTWORK
BLOCKCHAIN TECHNOLOGY

THE COMPREHENSIVE GUIDE

NFTs
DIGITAL
ARTWORK
BLOCKCHAIN
TECHNOLOGY

MARC BECKMAN

SKYHORSE PUBLISHING

To my very special wife and best friend, Alice.
And to my two amazing children, Jude and Damaris.

Author's Note

This is a book about a new and emerging technology. As such, it is almost certain that by the time you read these pages, the world of Non-Fungible Tokens (NFTs) will have changed. More specifically, it will have grown, evolved, and expanded into new areas, and in ways that include new players and technologies. The record prices for NFT works of art mentioned in this book may be broken. The largest and most lucrative partnerships with artists, athletes, and fashion brands to create NFTs may have been superseded and eclipsed. Businesses launching their own NFTs may—and, in fact, probably will—have accelerated at a remarkable pace since the time of this writing, and created NFT-based innovations and products that are not included here.

However, this is also a book about the basic, fundamental truths of NFTs—what they are, where and how they can be applied, and where they hold the potential to create powerful disruptions in our lives. These fundamentals will not change as time goes by. Rather, they will be used in exciting new ways, and in new areas, and this will be happening all the time . . . including after this book goes to press.

As champions of NFTs, we wouldn't have it any other way.

—Marc Beckman

Introduction

"What just happened?"

This was the question that seemed to echo across the art world—and then across the *entire* world—as news spread of a remarkable and unusual sale by Christie's auction house in early March of 2021. A digital collage entitled *Everydays: The First 5000 Days*, by an American artist known only as

Beeple, had sold for a staggering $69.3 million. The sale price alone made this transaction remarkable news. But there was something more. Something that took this transaction from the realm of the rare into the land of the positively game changing.

What had been sold by Christie's was not a canvas. Or a print. Or a sculpture. Or anything that could be touched or felt or held in someone's hand.

What had just sold for this staggering sum had come in the form of an NFT, or non-fungible token. Technically speaking, it was a digital file, but not just *any* digital file. The artwork contained a token verifying the unique nature of the piece, and tracing the record of the work's ownership back to the very circumstance of its creation. The token meant that the work could never be altered or changed by anyone save the new owner—who turned out to be a famous blockchain investor—and that no facsimile or reproduction of the work could ever truly be created, because any reproduction would lack this unique, distinguishing token.

Confused?

Many in the art world certainly were, at least initially. But this sense of bemusement was soon followed by a creeping feeling that something very important had just occurred—something with the potential to change transactions—and even the very notion of "ownership"—forever.

These are, after all, times of remarkable change . . . especially in the digital world.

The rise of cryptocurrency is revolutionizing how payments are executed, while at the same time building an entirely new class of investors. Crypto is also creating a world of finance and financial transactions that are free from government regulation in ways that have never before been possible. With the value of digital tokens like Bitcoin hitting middle five figures, even entities that had been skeptical of the utility of cryptocurrency (or who had downright called it a scam) are now changing their tunes and rushing to invest.

Stepping back for an even wider view, blockchain—the mechanism that underpins both cryptocurrency and NFTs—is advancing the technology used to verify who created something, who owns something (digital or otherwise), and where that something came from. With blockchain, the ownership history of a piece of currency is baked into the currency itself, and is accessible to anyone who examines it.

Imagine you could take a dollar out of your wallet and immediately know every person who had used that dollar, the nature of every transaction it'd been used for, and that you could see back to the very moment when the bill was printed.

In the real world, you can exchange a dollar bill with your friend for another dollar, and the contents of your respective wallets will be—for all practical purposes—essentially unchanged. Neither of your dollars is going to be more valuable than the other. And the history of both dollars essentially remains a mystery. You don't know where it came from, or how it has been used. And you probably have the same chance of being able to guess if the dollar is real, or if it has been counterfeited.

But not so with NFTs.

This is the "NF" part of an NFT. It's non-fungible. That means you can't exchange it for something like it somewhere else, and have everything be exactly as it was.

Many things of value are fungible, especially cash or coin money. But with the rise of crypto, that is going to change—for currency, but also for artworks, for collectibles, and for digital items of all sorts.

As the art world learned after the sale of Beeple's collage, an NFT is value because it is an utterly unique item, and this fact is verifiable. An NFT is a custodian of its own uniqueness. It can self-verify as a one-of-a-kind work of art. (Like a counterfeit detector can show that a bill is authentic, an NFT does this for itself.) An NFT can "tell its own story," and it can do that for as long as it exists.

Even to those unfamiliar with cryptocurrency or blockchain, with the sale of Beeple's collage, the puzzle pieces began to fall into place. Suddenly, the blockchain wasn't just for digital currencies like Bitcoin. Now, it was going to be for *all sorts of things*.

In the art world, the problem of fakes would disappear completely. The owner of a work could sell that work at any time, and have full faith in the transaction. Buyers would enjoy a new level of confidence in the authenticity of their new asset.

And then there was the existential side of things!

Purchasing artwork in the form of an NFT would create a deep and powerful level of ownership never before available to an art collector. The person purchasing a work of art as an NFT would have full claim not only to the work, but to its entire past, back to the moment of inception. Furthermore, that collector would always have an irrevocable place in the work's history regardless of who might come to own it in the future. Their name would be on its blockchain forevermore, and old notions of curation and custodianship would turn entirely on their heads.

And as the mind-boggling circumstances of the sale of *Everydays: The First 5000 Days* slowly began to become clear, entrepreneurs and professionals dealing in content creation began asking a new question. No longer was it, "What just happened?" but now it was, "So what about me?"

If NFTs could work in the world of fine art, then what about the world of sports imagery, or fashion photography, or music, or important historical documents? The list goes on and on.

It became clear that anything that was bought, sold, collected, or inherited stood to be impacted in a positive way by NFTs. Artists and photographers were about to find remarkable new revenue streams, and previously unimagined incarnations for their work. Brands were going to find new ways of connection with their customers. Entertainers and video game developers were going to immerse fans in ways never before dreamed of.

I wanted to write this book because, frankly, this powerful change is coming whether people like it or not. In an era when the disrupting and upending of entire industries has become a regular occurrence, negotiating the "NFT-transition" will be an important part of businesses staying competitive in the twenty-first century.

In this book, my goal is to provide you with a solid overview of NFTs, and to take away the "mystery" that some people felt when *Everydays: The First 5000 Days* was sold. I'll lay out NFTs' relationship to blockchain and digital currency to help you to understand how NFTs work precisely. We'll explore the nuts-and-bolts of how NFTs will help creators monetize their creative assets in exciting new ways, and how collectors can strike at the right time to invest in a completely original form of asset. Finally, I will help prepare you to *act now* in preparation for this new world just on the horizon.

It was one thing to explain what Bitcoin even *was* ten years ago, but quite another to forecast what Bitcoin would *mean*.

If you want to understand what happened in March of 2021, why it matters today, and how to position yourself for success in the world it's about to bring about, then read on . . .

PART ONE

Meet Your Guide

Who am I? How did I get involved in NFTs? And how did I come to be your personal Virgil, leading you through this strange and exotic new landscape?

I am best known as the founder of the award-winning agency, DMA United, which combines commercially oriented principles with branding and advertising. I like to say that DMA United operates "at the intersection of style and design." A small sampling of DMA United's clients includes the NBA, Karl Lagerfeld, MoMA, LVMH, Warner Brothers Entertainment, Sony Music, and the estate of Nelson Mandela.

I am also an attorney with a JD degree, and an adjunct professor at NYU Stern's MBA Program, where I serve as Co-Chair of NYU Stern's Luxury & Fashion Council. I live in New York City with my wife and two kids.

My pathway into NFTs hedged on a chance meeting.

It came down to an encounter with Stephane De Baets. Stephane works in finance, real estate, and hospitality. He's always been a really forward-thinking guy whom I respect immensely. On the fateful night, I'd caught up with Stephane at a restaurant he owns in SoHo called the Chefs Club. Ostensibly, we were there to explore doing some branding and advertising for the restaurant. We were discussing our shared passion for innovation and futurism, when Stephane told me he had recently purchased the St. Regis Hotel in Aspen "through blockchain."

Through blockchain? I thought. *How? Why?* But the more he told me, the more it became clear that there had been a method to his madness! The blockchain-backed aspect of the purchase had opened up new business possibilities. As he explained to me, Stephane had used the St. Regis as an asset to back the launch of a new crypto—the Aspen Digital Token, or AspenDigital—which let qualified investors take minority stakes in the property itself. Ultimately, this allowed about 20 percent of the hotel to be purchased and owned entirely by these minority investors. The other 80 percent stayed in the possession of Stephane's company. But that wasn't all. Holders of AspenDigital tokens were welcomed into a special rewards and privileges program that activated whenever they visited the property. Owners of even a small amount of AspenDigital would receive 20 percent cash back on all money spent during their stay at the St. Regis, and large coinholders could receive as much as 50 percent back.

I was blown away by what Stephane had done here. Not only had he democratized the investment process; he had allowed for even small players to own powerful investments that were 100 percent supported by blockchain. And in the same stroke, he was creating entirely new interactions with the property itself.

But, as I learned in the days to follow, Stephane wasn't yet finished . . .

When the COVID-19 pandemic hit, Stephane and I saw early-on that restaurants would be under tremendous strain, and many would simply not survive. This time, Stephane and I worked together, in a *pro bono* manner, to find ways that digital tokens could be used not only to support restaurant owners, but also to create a trickle-down effect that would reach the kitchen staff and gig economy workers. We developed a simple exchange by which a customer could enter a restaurant and pay $500 for a digital token that could be exchanged for $1,000 worth of dining in the future, after COVID-19. The extra $500 functioned like an advance that helped to keep kitchens afloat through the pandemic, and the model resulted in the creation of a new form of crypto focused on the restaurant community.

Needless to say, I became very intrigued by what I saw happening in blockchain and crypto—especially because it was going above and beyond what most people think of when they visualize a blockchain-backed transaction. These were innovators doing entirely new things and I started to explore how it might intersect with my world at DMA United.

Fashion, art, professional sports, social justice—all of this stood to be impacted by these new tools. In May of 2020, the concept of digital collectibles and unique brand ownership experiences led me to pilot Truesy—an NFT marketplace that really hit DMA United's community in its "sweet spot" where design, branding and fashion meet.

Now you know who I am. Next, I'll explain a little more about why I think blockchains are the best solution for the problems of today . . . and of tomorrow.

Blockchain and the problem of provenance

Blockchain is the technology that makes the NFT revolution possible, so understanding it is key.

Oftentimes, the easiest way to wrap your head around a complicated new invention is to start with the question: "What problem was this designed to solve?" When it comes to blockchain, the answer is the problem of provenance. That is, the history of ownership.

Blockchain is a digital "living ledger" that grows each time it is used for something. Generally, this "use" will be a financial transaction. Blockchain cannot be altered inappropriately, and it cannot be forged or counterfeited. A blockchain exists electronically, and requires a digital record—powered by a computer server—to maintain the integrity of its living ledger. Each time a transaction occurs, that transaction is recorded on this digital ledger. This ledger is transparent, so any participant in the technology can see it, and can verify that it happened. The transactions are also time-stamped and irreversible. (There are no "returns" in the world of blockchain. A transaction can't be reversed, recalled, or undone. Something can be sold and resold, but there is no "undo" button.) Blockchain transactions also have the quality of "unanimity"—that is to say, all participants in the network agree to the validity and binding nature of all blockchain transactions.

Blockchain transactions are secure because everyone involved in the chain is also involved in verifying the transactions. (This is sort of like if everyone using a physical piece of currency—like the US dollar—was also involved in checking bills for authenticity, and likewise making sure all bills were being legally used by the last person who had obtained them through a transaction.) Blockchain-backed currencies and tokens prevent forgery and fakery because of this kind of technological transparency. If someone tried to tamper with a block on a blockchain, every other user of the same blockchain would immediately know. This would be like if a counterfeiter bleached a $1 bill and reprinted the design of a $100 bill on top of it; everyone using that currency would immediately know. This is one reason that—although it runs on digital technology—a blockchain can't be "hacked" in the way a computer network can. Furthermore, most blockchain networks are getting bigger all the time, adding more users to the chain; this makes transactions on the chain safer and safer, because there are always more users who would notice if anything were amiss.

To best understand the technology, it may be helpful to consider blockchain's most prominent example, which is definitely Bitcoin. The blockchain that runs Bitcoin was created by a mysterious person (or persons) known as "Satoshi Nakamoto." In creating his cryptocurrency, Nakamoto devised a way that the history of each Bitcoin would be verified electronically with a digital timestamp, and a record of each Bitcoin would be maintained in an electronic ledger. What would power this ledger? The answer is Bitcoin mining.

Nakamoto designed his system such that the record of all Bitcoin transactions could be decentralized and maintained by a network of computers around the world that were actively "mining" Bitcoins. We use the word mining, but what these computers are actually doing is solving a series of complex mathematic problems that then maintain the chain of transactions in the Bitcoin ledger. (Why would anyone do this mining? Because the miners are rewarded periodically for this work with new Bitcoins of their own.) There are some downsides to this model, such as environmental implications—which we'll address—but as a system for maintaining the integrity of Bitcoin, this mass collaboration/verification model works well.

Bitcoin solves the problem of provenance, but it also does so much more. Bitcoins are not physical. They're not made of a substance that can be used for anything. They certainly can't be redeemed for gold (or other valuable metals), like some hard currencies can. Many of the advantages of Bitcoin, however, are in other things that they *can't* do. Namely, they can't be faked in any way. There is no such thing as a fake Bitcoin. Paper currency can be (and widely is) faked. When you pick up a $100 bill, you have no idea of its origins. You don't know if it was born in the US Mint or in a North Korean forgery operation. That information is not available to you as the person touching the currency. But with Bitcoin, that information is not only available, but it's an integral part of that piece of currency.

Alongside forgery is theft. A pickpocket can steal money from your wallet and then spend it freely without a merchant being any the wiser. Bitcoins are not possible to "steal" in the traditional sense of the word because the record of ownership transactions is imprinted on the blockchain.

Bitcoin is also free from any risks that come from being tied to a government or central regulatory entity. For example, a government can suddenly declare that a currency note can be redeemed for—and is therefore "worth"—$100 in gold. Or $200. Or is suddenly *no longer* redeemable for the thing that formerly backed it. When governments do this, it can cause inflation, deflation, currency manipulation, and general chaos across the board. But a Bitcoin is redeemable for nothing physical, and is always worth whatever people are willing to pay for it. And it is incredibly liquid and easy to sell or convert. A government can also gradually devalue currency whenever it sees fit by printing more money. Bitcoin, to the contrary, cannot be devalued in this way because a unique and finite number of Bitcoins has already been set. After the remaining Bitcoins are mined, there will never been new ones added to circulation. (This quality of finality and uniqueness will come into play as we look more deeply at the advantages of NFTs.)

Finally, Bitcoin solves the problem of central authority *by keeping government almost totally out of the picture.* (Though not completely. It should be noted that certain governments have outright banned the trading of cryptocurrencies like Bitcoin.) Bitcoins are unique, and when they are yours, they can stay yours forever. But a government, if it so wishes, can recall all its currency notes and replace them with newly-issued, updated ones. When you own physical money issued by a government, there is always the possibility—however small—that that same government can issue new laws or rulings that will impact your physical money in a negative way.

This kind of tension is also felt where the worlds of art and money intersect—a spot where blockchain technology and NFTs will be centrally important. In the art world, a repressive government might declare a painting or other artwork to be obscene, "antirevolutionary," or otherwise treasonous—and so outlaw or confiscate it. Imagine if a beautiful and expensive work of art were suddenly declared illegal to own! But when assets are owned electronically and as non-physical manifestations, the government's ability to physically seize a unit of currency or piece of art becomes a much trickier prospect. Enforcement of these kind of repressive rules would be incredibly difficult for a government to actually implement.

In summary, a blockchain is a self-preserving digital ledger that keeps records of everything on the ledger, and all legitimate reactions related to it. It solves the problem of

Rick and Morty *creator Justin Roiland made over $1 million for an NFT comprised of a crudely-drawn sketch of character from* The Simpsons *nude.*

provenance, counterfeiting, and all kinds of physical deception. When used to back a currency, it also takes great steps to prevent inappropriate government interference and regulation.

If that's blockchain, then what is an NFT?

Put simply, an NFT is a digital token backed by blockchain—just like a Bitcoin is. However, an NFT also represents a unique digital file—as opposed to a unit of currency—and this digital file usually takes the form of visual artwork, a GIF, an audio file, or something similar.

Another way to think about it is that an NFT is a piece of digital art, video, or audio that is tied to the blockchain like a unit of cryptocurrency. Yet while units of the same cryptocurrency are all technically unique, they are also all worth the same amount. (You can go online right now and look up how much a Bitcoin is worth. That number will be the going rate for *all* Bitcoins.) NFTs may be backed by the same blockchain, but in most cases they are going to be worth *different* amounts of money—just as though they were unique works of art. *Because they are.*

And just like a work of art, a digital NFT art piece won't have a "going rate" you can look up, like you can look up the price of a Bitcoin. There'll be a record of the purchase price of your NFT, but if you want to find out how much you can get for it *now*, you'll have to auction it off or put it up for sale some other way. (There will also be rules of thumb relating to certain artists that experts will be able to issue. For example, what does an early Salvador Dalí oil painting typically go for? Or a late-stage Cézanne? Art world experts will be able to provide very educated guesses, but we'll still never know for certain until the painting actually goes on sale.)

Thinking of NFTs as "unique digital works of art, like paintings or videos" is necessary but not sufficient. That is to say, the art world is where NFTs seem to have "broken through" first. But as you'll see later in this book, there are going to be massive applications across all kinds of industries for digital representations that enjoy all the benefits of being tied to a blockchain.

Musician Casey Spooner released a music video as an NFT.

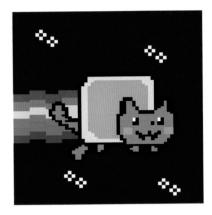

When I buy an NFT, what exactly am I buying?

When most people ask this question, they are again referring to an NFT that's a work of digital art, so let's start there.

An art collector purchasing an NFT buys a unique and secure digital token—backed by blockchain—representing ownership of that digital work of art. Put plainly, you get one digital file. The file contains a copy of the artwork, and it's also tied to the blockchain.

Seems simple, right? But, as you might imagine, to reduce NFT art to these details sort of misses the point. There's much more to it, which becomes apparent when you understand that upon purchasing the NFT, your doing so enters the blockchain and *becomes a part of the NFT itself.*

To put it another way, when you buy an NFT, you buy *the fact that you have bought the NFT.* The fact of your doing so is secured on the history of that NFT for all time, and this fact becomes verifiable by anyone, anywhere, as part of the blockchain.

You own the digital file. You own it forever (or at least until you sell it). And anyone on the blockchain will be able to verify that fact at any time.

Another useful question is: What *don't* you buy when you buy an NFT?

Well, you don't own the rights to the work, or to representations of it; that copyright still rests with the creator/artist. (If you bought the copyright *in addition* to the NFT, then you would also own these things. However, most purchasers of NFT art do not do this.) Buying an NFT is more like buying a digital work of art with a unique serial number. It is up to the artist or creator how many NFTs like yours exist. A good analogy might be a limited-edition baseball card, or wristwatch, or print reproduction of a painting. Yours may be "1 of 100" or "1 of 1." The important thing is—just like baseball cards, or watches, or prints—it is unique and can still go up in value, still be sold, and still be traded. It also has the unique advantage of authenticity that is backed by the blockchain.

Is this a new and different sort of art collecting? Absolutely. But so is everything important when it first comes on the scene. Remember: NFTs are not "better" or "worse" to own than traditional forms of art. They are a new way to own art entirely.

Contemporary artist Takashi Murakami has explored numerous aspects of NFTs, including copyright implications for the artist.

Where will my NFT "be" and how can I see it?

Technically speaking, your NFT will exist on a blockchain supported by a server. For as long as the blockchain exists, your NFT will exist.

Artist Urs Fischer created tension between himself and his art dealer by launching NFTs, but ultimately found the transition extremely lucrative.

In the case of NFTs that take the form of still images or video clips, you will be able to view your NFT wherever you have a screen or device on which to display it. How people "see" your NFT will largely be up to you.

But just because an NFT won't "be" in your house hanging on the wall, doesn't mean that it won't be yours, or won't be secure. (It can hang on your wall, if you wish, and be seen through a television screen, etc.) To the contrary, your NFT artwork may literally be the most secure thing that you own. It will almost definitely be the most secure work of art that you own. As we've seen, because the blockchain technology in NFTs literally imprints the history *of* the work *on* the work, authentication and provenance can be known instantly. Even with the carbon-dating of canvases, and the discerning eyes of trained art historians, forgeries and fakes can still be passed off as the real thing in the work of physical art. (Or a stolen painting may be "found" years later after a questionable chain of ownership.) But when a piece of art is an NFT, this possibility is eliminated completely.

The NFT will "be" on the blockchain, but it will also be yours however you wish to exhibit it.

So then how did we get from blockchain to NFT art?

Did NFTs begin with Beeple? Certainly not. Finding the precise origins of NFTs can be somewhat difficult. Unique digital items have been around for a few years. But when did one of these unique digital items cross the line from a commodity into "art"?

This, of course, begs the bigger question "What is art?" to which, there is no easy answer. Can digital currency—like the Bitcoins that preceded NFTs—count as art?

Actually, maybe they can.

Money has been used in (or as) art many times before, and several artists have simply exhibited physical piles of currency as artworks in galleries. In 2017, artist Danai Anesiadou sealed a kilogram of gold in plastic and declared that it was a piece of art. And back in 1994, Bill Drummond and Jimmy Cauty performed an "art piece" in which they burned a million British pounds in currency notes in a fire.

Had forms of digital currency already functioned as art, prior to NFTs? It's possible. (And is something art historians will surely debate in years to come.) However, most in the space agree that the first proper works of digital NFT art were

CryptoPunks by Larva Labs have sold for millions of dollars.

13

probably CryptoPunks, closely followed by CryptoKitties, which premiered in late November of 2017. CryptoKitties was (and still is) an Ethereum-based blockchain game that allows users to collect and breed digital cats. Through the robust CryptoKitties online community, users could create their own unique cats—which exist forever as NFTs—and trade them with and sell them to one another. Within the first week of its launch, users of CryptoKitties purchased over $1M of these digital cat images!

While online cats might seem a bit unserious as the progenitors of a massive artistic revolution, people were buying these cats for the same reasons that anybody buys fine art. The images were nice to look at. Buying them was fun. You could make money from them because you were purchasing an appreciating asset. It was a way to show that you were "in the know" and "cultured" (or at least "online cultured"). And it was a way of expressing your interests while supporting artists financially.

CryptoKitties also showed one of the defining and revolutionary features of NFT art in that it was accessible to collectors at almost any level of wealth. The most modestly priced CryptoKitty NFTs started at just $12.

Sensing (correctly) that these cat NFTs were just the opening notes in the great symphony of collectible digital art, developers quickly set to work creating online marketplaces where NFTs could be bought and sold—and where artists new to the space could have their creations turned into NFTs. In 2018, a number of NFT marketplaces such as SuperRare, OpenSea, Nifty Gateway, and MakersPlace, were up and running.

In most cases, these NFT marketplaces make money by taking a percentage of each NFT sold. In return, they get the NFTs in front of the eyes of buyers, and facilitate the transactions.

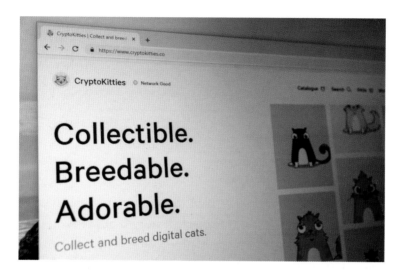

With the rise of these online marketplaces, even more players started to get in the game. Literally. One of the most prominent entities to join the NFT space after CryptoKitties was the NBA's official platform for selling game highlights—NBA Top Shot. In its first half-year operation, NBA Top Shot has done approximately $400 million in business!

The success of NBA Top Shot is important because it showed that a community of fans who might not be tech-inclined would take the steps to become so if it meant they could engage with their favorite sport in an exciting new way. Another, similar example would be the rock band Kings of Leon releasing an album in early 2021 as an audio NFT. Their fans were willing to make the leap to NFT, and the album made millions of dollars for the band.

The story of the journey from blockchain to NFTs can also be seen in the way we're watching NFTs change the nature of art collecting as a financial venture—especially when it comes to how works can be resold. To cite just one prominent example, a group of art collectors calling themselves Metapurse purchased twenty NFT artworks by Beeple in January of 2021. They then fractionalized their ownership of the works into tokens, and then they made those tokens available for sale to the public. Thousands of people bought them. Going by the value of the tokens at the time of this writing, the twenty works of art have now increased in value approximately six-fold.

Try doing *that* with a Rembrandt.

Everyone's getting into the act. Bhad Bhabie, a.k.a. the "Cash Me Outside" girl, has auctioned 20 NFTs based on her famous meme.

So now, we're at this point where there seems to be endless opportunity and continual innovation as we see blockchain connecting in new ways with the technology.

At least for the moment, there appears to be an endless appetite for NFT products. And even fan bases that may not be "into tech" are proving willing to take the leap to get to NFTs. But with this success comes legitimate questions about where NFTs will go next. Artists are constantly experimenting with new forms of art that can be created virtually. Developers are thinking about what else can be sold virtually (or sold as an NFT). For example, there is a booming market in virtual NFT real estate. You might not be able to own a mansion in real life, but now users can purchase one in a virtual world. We're also seeing collectors scramble to figure out the best ways to exhibit their NFTs. Businesses are doing this too as they wish to develop and launch their own unique NFT products. And when you have a product, you want to get it in front of the eyes of your customers. But *who are your customers* and *how are they going to find your NFTs*? That's what we're still figuring out.

From this evolving landscape, a solid piece of wisdom has already emerged: Don't bet against NFTs. People who said that NFTs would remain small and niche were wrong. Those who claimed that only people who worked in the tech industry would ever purchase NFTs were also demonstrably incorrect. And those who claimed that NFTs "might be well and good for the unwashed tech-proletariat" but "we'll never see those things being sold by the great auction houses for millions of dollars?" You guessed it; also wrong.

What walls are NFTs going to break through next? While nobody can predict the future for certain, in this book we'll identify top candidates for places that NFTs will probably take off next.

And one day, far in the future, in a marketplace where NFTs are so common they hardly raise an eyebrow, we may look back in amusement knowing that it seems to have all started with collectible digital cats.

Are there any areas of controversy within crypto, blockchain, and NFTs?

Blockchain technology has seen its fair share of skepticism and criticism. At this point, I suppose we should be used to it!

Since the dawn of time, new inventions and innovations have given rise to confusion regarding the unfamiliar new product. In some unfortunate cases, this has set the stage for consumers making purchases in which they did not fully understand what they were buying—or even for outright fraud.

The good news is that blockchain-backed technology is becoming more familiar to everyone, including people who may not be on the leading edge of tech (or tech savvy at all). The essentials of what blockchain is and how it works are getting out there. Everyone has heard of Bitcoin—which is a start—even if they don't know how it works or how to buy it. While there is still the potential for miscommunication, an increasingly educated consumer base means that in general there is less confusion around blockchain technology.

The even better news is that, when it comes to NFTs, their unique technology is providing a strong counter to much of the criticism that their predecessors experienced.

Cryptocurrencies like Bitcoin, for example, have long been criticized for their energy consumption and carbon footprint. How can a digital coin—that you can't even hold or touch—have a carbon footprint in the "real world"? The answer is: because Bitcoin maintains its blockchain by mining, the miners will always need electricity to power the computers doing the mining. As Bitcoin has grown—and more and more of the coins have been mined—the cost of mining has accelerated ever upward. A study by the University of Cambridge published in early 2021 reported that, globally, Bitcoin mining now uses approximately as much electricity each year as the country of Argentina. All of this power use raises the specter of carbon emissions and elevates the carbon footprint of Bitcoin. And alas, most of the energy powering Bitcoin mining does not yet come from renewable sources (even though Bitcoin enthusiasts are promising that this is soon going to change). The good news is that contemporary NFTs can be produced in ways that have only the smallest fraction of the environmental impact of something like a Bitcoin (again, more on this later.) If they are rolled out the right way, NFTs won't have to create the energy drain that Bitcoins do.

Other criticisms of blockchain products have come from enabling "pump and dump" schemes, or schemes in which a cryptocurrency with no value has been launched to intentionally dupe newcomers. For example, as the value of Bitcoin slowly but steadily began to increase in the early 2010s, the cryptocurrency market became flooded with new "coins" launched every week. Many of the creators of these new coins were just out to make a quick buck. To make this fast money, they might launch a crypto in connection to a meaningless gimmick—"The new alt-coin for parakeet lovers, which everyone with a parakeet will want to use!"—and then a billion coins would be released. Half would be put up for sale on a crypto exchange, but half would be retained by the creators of the coin. If the value of that new coin reached just one cent, for example, the creators of the coin could sell their half a billion

ParakeetCoin, clear $20M out of thin air, and walk away. Coinholders (and parakeet lovers everywhere) would feel duped and taken advantage of.

But NFTs tied to works of art, iconic images, and other unique and meaningful content present an entirely new arrangement, and eliminate the possibility of a creator seeking to quickly and anonymously "cash out." It's an entirely different proposition. The ownership chain is clear. Those selling the NFT do so in an environment of transparency. Potential buyers can research who sellers are, and can work to genuinely understand the product being offered. The value, the integrity, and the uniqueness of the item being purchased as an NFT is assured.

Other areas of controversy have also arisen from copyright violation. This is a problem in just about every visual media. While copyright violation appears to be rare in the world of NFT art, there have been a few documented cases. For example, in early 2021, both CNN and VICE reported on artists claiming that someone had copied one of their original digital artworks and sold it as an NFT without permission. When this happens, the original artist is forced to pursue a copyright claim. With the number of NFTs for sale expanding exponentially, this type of violation will probably keep occurring. However, the good news is that because the technology is digital, it will be much easier to 1) report the offense, 2) locate the bad actor, and 3) ensure that the problematic NFT is dealt with appropriately. When an artist alleges their work has been copied and sold without permission in the physical world, there can be a great deal of (slow and tedious) work to determine exactly who was involved and where all the inappropriate copies are. In the digital world, this kind of problem—once users become aware of it—can be remedied much more quickly, and the location of any illicit work is never in question. In the meantime, security for visual artists will continue to evolve so that inappropriate use is prevented. (For example, when displaying their work on their own websites, many visual artists now use a "floating banner" that always obscures a small portion of their work. This prevents it from being digitally captured.)

To conclude, blockchain technology is not new to criticism. However, the earliest critics of technologies like cryptocurrency have gradually had over a decade to be proved wrong. The criticisms being leveled at NFTs now are few, are much less daunting than what cryptos faced, and there is every reason to feel confident that evolving technology will allow us to solve any problems that might arise as we move forward.

Now the ball is rolling . . .

At the time of this writing, most people are still thinking of digital works of visual art when they think of NFTs—and that's totally fine—but, as I mean to make clear in this book, that incarnation only scratches the surface of what the technology is going to make possible. Massive moves are underway at this very moment to expand what NFTs can do. They are happening in the background and out of view of most people, but they are definitely there. Businesses and creators everywhere are rushing to prepare for a brave new world of NFTs in art and commerce.

NFTs are digital files, so just about anything comported digitally can be an NFT. For example, a concert ticket or a plane ticket can be an NFT. A digital discount code can be an NFT. A digital receipt can be an NFT. Utilitarian NFTs are going to be useful for cultivating relationships between brands, creators, and consumers.

When it comes to digital items, the question really isn't "What can be an NFT?" but rather "Is there anything that *can't* be an NFT?"

Just as it is difficult to imagine a world without omnipresent internet or smartphones, soon it will be hard for us to recall a time *before* there were NFTs. There is momentum building, and it's not going away.

Grimes made $5.8M in a matter of minutes selling original NFT art.

We're seeing it in the art world first, yes—according to *TIME* magazine, in the first two months of 2021, nearly $250M was spent on NFTs *not counting* Beeple's record-setting sale at Christie's—but an entire economy has begun to develop to support the integration of NFTs into other areas of our lives. Other products. Other services.

There are businesses that can help creators "mint" their NFTs, but also platforms to assist in the sale of NFTs, valuers to help artists and investors understand the fair price of these digital pieces, and consultants to help collectors curate their collections.

Luxury brands are asking themselves how a luxury purchase can include an NFT that then "unlocks" further high-end experiences, unique services, access to new merch launches, collaborations, etc. Sports companies are preparing for massive growth in the digital space that will be fueled by NFTs. And companies of all sorts that are customer-facing are preparing to connect directly with those future customers somewhere along the digital blockchain.

Businesses realize that the very lexicon itself has expanded. As people trend toward the "authentic" and "true," buyers will increasingly want to own the genuine and unique version of something. Just as uniqueness exists in the physical world, so too will it now exist in the digital one.

With more and more people discovering this format every day, it's going to be well-nigh impossible to "put the toothpaste back in the tube." NFTs are here to stay.

In the next section we'll explore the types of NFTs businesses and brands are creating, and look at where we can expect those NFTs to create the most opportunity.

NFT art by creator Hashmask has sold for over $800,000.

PART TWO

An NFT . . . but
What Kind of NFT

We're already seeing how NFTs will present a revolution for fine artists, brands, luxury fashion designers, elite athletes, musicians, and entertainers. We are forging new partnerships with clients excited to move into the space. Even prior to the writing of this book, our client list included Warner Brothers Entertainment, Barney's New York, MoMA, and the NBA.

The work we've done so far can serve as a guide to the kind of NFT opportunities that are out there for major brands and creators.

In this section, we'll look at some of the choices brands face when they are thinking about how to implement NFTs in their area of growth.

To begin, let's look at the very first choice brands have to make.

———————

Static or dynamic

NFTs have the ability to function as tokens that can be recognized at digital points of contact with a brand.

Think about how such a thing could be used in the world of, say, retail . . .

This NFT? It will entitle you to 10 percent off in any of our retail boutiques.

That NFT? It will function as your entrance ticket to our exclusive secret event for our best customers.

This other NFT? It lets us contact you when we have breaking news about updates for that product you bought. In fact, the NFT is embedded in the product.

But first, it's helpful to understand that NFTs come in two types: Static and Dynamic.

"Static" for our purposes means an NFT that is self-contained. It does *not* necessarily mean "unmoving." Static NFTs can take the form of still images, yes, but they can also include 3D, animated, VR, AR, GIFs, short videos, etc. They can also include audio elements (sounds), or be completely silent. So a picture, a video, or an audio file NFT can all be Static NFTs.

Static NFTs usually create revenue by generating money for their creator in their initial sale. (They can also create revenue in perpetuity with each future transaction, if such a condition is specified on the blockchain. For example, it's specified that each time the NFT is sold, the creator gets 5 percent of that sale price.)

Static NFTs include NFTs sold as fine art. So when most people today use the term "NFT," they are typically referring to a Static NFT. When you're looking at (or listening to) a Static NFT, then what you're experiencing is the whole width and breadth of what it is and what it does. It will forever be that—no more, no less. It may *move*—if it's animated, for example—but it never *changes*.

Artists like WhisBe have found considerable success with NFTs containing animations.

Dynamic NFTs are different.

Dynamic NFTs bring all the same initial qualities of Static NFTs (they may be video, animated, VR, pictures, GIFs, music, etc.), but they have the capacity to be updated through an additional connection. It may be a connection back to the original artist or business that created the NFT, or it may simply connect to a network that allows it to be updated according to preset rules. With a Dynamic NFT, the digital asset remains responsive to (and connected to) the issue's original design, messaging, and conditions.

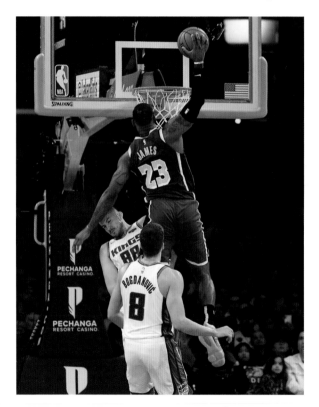

Here's an example of the distinction. A Static NFT of a LeBron James basketball card would contain his lifetime stats *up to the moment that the NFT was created,* and those stats would never change as LeBron continued to play new games. A Dynamic NFT of the same basketball card could be programmed to always update a basketball card whenever LeBron played another NBA game, continually keeping current.

A Dynamic NFT can also be programmed to act in concert *with other NFTs.* For example, an NFT of a baseball card might be programmed to have one background color—or one animation—as individual members of a professional team are gradually collected. But when that collector buys *all* the NFTs of the entire roster of a certain team, the NFT could "notice" this and change to an entirely new background color in recognition of the achievement.

Dynamic NFTs can also be synced to capture and preserve information about the users themselves . . .

Consider a video game with a Dynamic NFT. It could constantly update each time the user gets a new high score. (And any dragons slain and maidens rescued could be preserved on the blockchain forever!)

Consider an automobile owner. If a Dynamic NFT were connected to the car's vitals, then when it came time for resale, there would be no question about how long the car had been owned, where it had been driven, and how frequently the oil had been changed. All this information would be irrevocably preserved on the blockchain.

Or what about integrating a Dynamic NFT with a fitness app/tracker? A jogger's fastest time, max heart rate, or number of steps per day could be preserved on an NFT that would update each time the athlete hit a new personal best.

A Dynamic asset provides ongoing engagement with the issuer, and also holds the potential for ongoing transaction functionalities.

Right now, when the general public thinks of NFTs, they think of Static NFTs. All the thinkpieces in magazines are about NFTs functioning as collectible works of art. But what's happening behind the scenes and out of view is the laying of the groundwork for a whole world of these Dynamic NFTs.

To be clear, this doesn't mean that Static NFTs are going to go away. As you'll see in the following sections, both Static and Dynamic NFTs are going to work together to create opportunities for artists, businesses, and brands.

Static NFTs as part of a comprehensive branded environment

Brands stand to be positively changed by the rise of NFTs (both kinds). In the 21st century, brands are becoming more multifaceted and dynamic, and the very definition of what (or even who) qualifies as a brand has been changing rapidly.

Historically, a "brand" was defined as anything that denoted a product had been made by (or sold by) a certain business. This is an ancient, primal definition. (Think about the physical "branding" of cattle that's been going on for millennia.)

Today, however, branding goes far beyond the Nike swoosh on your shoe. It includes nearly every aspect of the brand's identity, activity, and performance. It can include advertising, endorsements, marketing and communication pieces, loyalty programs, and more. Yet the one constant in all of these elements will always be *product differentiation*. There's always something that makes your brand different from all the others. Something that makes it *special* and *desirable*.

When it is correctly cultivated, a brand becomes worth more than the sum of its parts. Customers come to value a particular brand favorably, and it can take on a life (and value) of its own. There are many cases of "zombie brands" in which a business may have long since gone under, but their symbol continues to be an integral part of the culture.

Next, consider the phrase "on brand." Then consider how frequently the phrase is used regarding things *outside of physical good*. A politician's speech is said to be "on brand." A singer's new album? "On brand" (or not, depending on the music). "Brand" comes to refer to an expected aspect of a product or service that satisfies customers in a way they expect, whether or not it is a physical good.

A business, a political party, even a person, can be a brand.

NFTs hold the potential to add to the ways in which brands can express themselves, connect with customers and fans, and define their own identities. NFTs can tell consumers more about the brand, identify the benefits of the product, express brand values or beliefs, or simply comport a sense of the brand's personality and sense of itself.

We've seen firsthand how NFTs can be seamlessly incorporated into an artist's or business's existing brand. We frequently work with brands to help ensure that they optimize their NFTs in order to have the biggest impact in the marketplace. Here, we'll outline some of this work to give you a sense of how Static NFTs are integrated with preexisting brands.

When we help a client who is expanding into the NFT marketplace, we work with them to create a standalone branded gallery environment. This is a "central hub" where potential customers and supporters can come to view the NFT content. This virtual gallery looks like an extension of the creator's brand. It doesn't feel like the customer is going to an online art gallery, or to an "outside source" of some kind. Rather, from the moment they click, visitors understand that they are still in a space that's a part of the brand itself.

The design of the Static NFTs themselves should also carry the branding of the business. However, this is general advice, and always remains general. The businesses should feel that it's up to them to determine how this branding will work. Businesses are tremendously protective over their branding, and have in-house brand custodians in their marketing and communications departments. These folks will be passionate about overseeing that branding is correctly and appropriately deployed in a piece of content like an NFT.

Our partners feel comfortable working with us because they retain full creative control. And at the end of the day, they have the final say.

We can also help the client understand that although it's a new technology, the NFT is not an exotic "other" that will be some kind of curveball for their branding department to deal with. Rather, the NFT can be a familiar extension of whatever they already make. They may produce physical collectible content items—like baseball cards or figurines—or they may simply have existing branding that can be worked into a collectible Static NFT. For example, an automobile company doesn't usually view its products as "collectible"—except by the very wealthy—but they will have strong branding across all platforms. This brand identity can be incorporated easily into something like collectible NFTs featuring popular cars.

When it's time for a business to offer their Static NFTs for the first time, we want to make that an event! Right now, it's not challenging to get the launch of NFTs into the news because there's so much interest in the new technology. But as the novelty wanes, what will be more important will be helping to ensure that a company's core customer group is made aware of the NFTs. We want them to understand how to access and collect the NFTs, but it's also important that we help customers see how NFTs can function as an extension of their fandom and enthusiasm for the product.

The most prominent NFTs are showcased and shown in their own environments. This is also (obviously) the case whenever a creator or brand has a single NFT for sale. If an NFT is important enough, then everything about the announcement and the sale will be tailored in service to that NFT.

We also help ensure clients launch their NFT on a selected schedule that's optimized through our relationship with our

creator. Timing is everything, and we let our clients understand not just how and where, but *when* to release their NFT.
An NFT launch can coincide with the launch of another new
product. It can be used as part of a larger campaign to signal a brand's commitment to twenty first–century technology. It can also introduce an important new revenue stream.
We work to ensure brands enjoy the benefit of optimal timing
in the marketplace.

And at the highest level, we listen to our clients. We learn
what they're hoping to achieve. We learn what makes their
customers feel passion for their products. And we help them
determine how their launch of an NFT can integrate with the
rest of their brand and contribute to overall awareness.

―――――――――――――――――――

Creating value for the client with a dynamic NFT

Another one of our central tasks is to assist any client in max-
imizing the value of a Dynamic NFT program that can help
them grow their brand.

Just a few examples of this work include:

- **Incorporating rewards programs:** Does our client
  want holders of their NFTs to receive discounts at a
  business? Should customers with NFTs accrue redeemable rewards points? The possibilities are wide
  open. We help our partners think long-term about
  the ways that NFTs can let customers build ev-
  er-stronger relationships with their brand.

- **Providing a fanbase with access to unique experiences:** For someone like a musician, Dynamic NFTs
  can function as digital keys that unlock special experiences, like a concert or art opening. The NFT

can make the fan aware of a special event, while at the same time serving as the admission pass to get inside. These NFTs can create a sense of exclusivity for "superfans" that make them feel closer to the artists they enjoy.

- **Providing a fanbase with access to unique services:** At many good restaurants, there's a special menu for those "in the know"—and then there's the regular menu for everyone else. Just as it can serve as a passport that opens up special event access, an NFT can also open up access to a whole new menu of products and services. Consumers who connect with a brand by purchasing an NFT are likely to be very committed to the brand, and therefore more likely to be interested in additional special services.

- **Providing a fanbase with access to limited edition product drops:** In the same vein as the above, NFT holders will be among the most likely to snap up special, limited edition productions that a brand may provide. The fact that those without the Dynamic NFT will not even know these offerings exist can create an optimal sense of FOMO that drives business for these special offerings (and drives it directly to the community that will be most likely to buy).

- **Leveraging technology for in-community communications:** Among the most exciting offerings of a Dynamic NFT is fostering connections within your fanbase community that can help improve brand awareness, and also help people who purchase your NFT to make the transition from "customer" to "fan of the brand." Just about every brand wants to foster fan communities and help them grow. By helping to ensure that NFTs function as "keys" to unlock admission to brand communities, we help ensure that fans connect with other fans, and help that fandom grow.

Obviously, there's a lot here, and not every part of this Dynamic NFT menu suits every partner we work with. But if you want to skip ahead, Part Four of this book contains more specific examples of how NFTs are being used (and will be used in the future) by different industries.

Empowering artists, creators, and investors together

One of the most exciting and satisfying parts of my job right now is knowing that we're going to be a part of a powerful new force that will help people get paid for doing something they love.NFTs are going to allow a new wave of artists and creators to make a living through art. And at the same time, artists and brands are going to be able to use technology to engage with their fans in ways that were literally undreamed of just a generation ago. A direct and personal relationship with the fan, with the consumer, with the owner of the art.

NFTs are going to create a new "layer" of artwork. That is to say, we're going to add an entirely new item to the list of resultant content involved with a work of art. There is the original work, there are photographic reproductions of the work, there are signed prints of the work, there are officially licensed replicas—and so on—and, now, there is the NFT.

Artist Naomi Osaka has released a number of works as NFTs.

Right away, this gives many artists and content creators a new revenue stream because it gives them something new to sell. For example, a painter paints a painting. She may sell the physical painting, she may license various reproductions of the painting as the copyright holder, and now she also may sell the NFT.

Some work is created digitally, and it has sometimes been a challenge for digital artists to make the case that their "original" is as legitimate, unique, and saleable as something painted with oil on canvas. Here too, giving digital artists the ability to sell an utterly unique NFT of their work, with its originality and provenance built into the blockchain, has the power to make meaningful transformative change for artists.

And while original paintings on canvas might still run into the problem of forgeries and fakes, as we've noted, NFTs will present the public with a work which is utterly "un-fakeable."

If you think about it, this will likely increase the value of NFTs compared to comparable works of physical art that *can* be forged. The media is full of thrilling tales of art forgers fooling experts. Whenever a painting or similar physical work of art comes up for sale—even when offered by a very reputable firm—there is always a non-zero chance that the work may not be authentic. We know from history that art buyers are always taking a risk. But what if there were no risk? No risk *at all*? This is what NFTs will bring to the table, and it's also a reason why NFTs will be able to command a price that doesn't carry that "baked in" possibility that a work might not be genuine. This is a tangible benefit, and it adds to the value of NFTs in the eyes of collectors. (Just think . . . You can be a collector of physical art pieces and be reasonably sure that *most* of the pieces in your collection are genuine, or you can be a collector of NFTs and be absolutely sure. Which sounds like a more attractive area in which to invest?)

NFT's will also empower creators by eliminating many of the barriers and intermediaries between the artist and their customer. The artist will be able to sell NFTs directly to the consumer. They will be only minimally subject to any form of corporate control. Government control will likewise be very limited. Local attempts at art censorship, for example, will not last long in the age of the NFT; they can too easily be circumvented.

NFTs will also bring to bear an entirely new aesthetic and digital canvas with which creators can experiment. It's only once in a great while that an invention or innovation allows that to happen. Photography. Film and moving images. Digital photography and digital canvasses. And now NFTs. With each new creation, artists took the technology and made great art. They expanded the media itself and used it in new ways. We'll forecast here and now that the next decade will see creators, artists, and brands beginning to curate works of art for optimization as an NFT in ways we can't even imagine now. Literally and figuratively, NFTs are a brand new canvas upon which a new generation of artists will learn to paint.

This will be viewable also in the unique aspects of NFTs connected to their evolution over time, and their ability to interact with other NFTs. Because it is digital and backed by the blockchain, nothing stops an artist from designing an NFT that changes physically each time it is sold. Or bid upon. Or gifted to someone. Or inherited. Likewise, as digital entities NFTs will have the potential ability to interact with other NFTs. Imagine a canvas that begins life as one color, but changes when the owner also owns a different NFT by the same artist. As an art collector purchases NFT after NFT from the same collection, the collector's digital canvas might continue to update and change. Or it might not. This is just one of the fun technical possibilities that will be available to artists.

The rise of the NFT will also have numerous impacts in areas like equity and civil rights. One way it will do this is by disrupting the current centralized access points for artists, which have resulted in a very homogenous landscape from which—even today—many diverse voices appear to be excluded. For example, according to the research paper "Glass Ceilings in the Art Market" posted in the *Social Science Research Network* (*SSRN*) in February of 2020, over 96 percent of artwork sold at auction is produced by men. There are still very few women artists represented in the most lucrative art sales. And research from CUNY's Guttman College conducted in 2016 found that just over 80 percent of artists represented in top New York City galleries are white. When that same Guttman College survey looked at only US-born artists, it found that 88 percent were white. The same study also found that artists in top New York galleries are overwhelmingly represented by graduates from a small handful of selective (and expensive) colleges and universities, virtually all of which are located in Los Angeles, Chicago, or along the Eastern Seaboard. When it comes to gender, race, and economic and geographic diversity, we can do better. Frankly, we *must* do better. If the art world is not profoundly embarrassed by this situation, it should be. NFTs can help make positive change happen by moving art away from being something curated by a small and insular group of elites. NFTs will be open and available in online virtual galleries accessible to anyone, anywhere with a computer. There will be no geographical limitations that keep an artist from a rural or Southern location in the US from having their work seen—while someone in New York has easy access. There will be no need for a gallery scene in one location to dominate. In short, NFTs will present an opportunity for a new, level playing field. Not only will this hopefully lead to a more diverse and gender-balanced group of prominent artists, but it will also allow artists across income levels and geographies to have a greater chance of making a living by selling their art.

Things will be better for art collectors too. NFTs will make art collecting possible for demographics who might never before have seen themselves in that role. Consider what (and who) one typically thinks of when the term "art collector" is used. It's someone with the means to purchase fine art, but also more than that. It is someone who may be relying on expert "sherpas" to guide them to the work that is likely to be the best investment. It's someone with the physical space to store the art that's being purchased (either in an appropriately stately manse, or in a climate controlled storage facility). We picture a person in a living situation secure enough that they are not too worried that their collected pieces will be stolen off their walls. We picture someone close enough to the nexus of art sales that—should they decide to part with a work of art—a sale to many qualified potential buyers can be arranged. Contrast this with the world of the potential collection of an NFT enthusiast. Because the work is presented digitally—and can be purchased from anywhere, by anyone—the NFT collector does not need to live among connected coastal elites, or know the right places and people to buy from. Anyone, anywhere can discover the next great NFT artist online. And artists and entities selling NFTs will have no reason to turn down a transaction once an offer on a work is made. They may not even have that ability. (In the world of fine art, art dealers know that *who* has purchased a work by a living artist will have the potential to impact the price of subsequent pieces by the same artist. Thus, art dealers wishing to see the market value of a certain artist's work ascend hope foremost that the work is purchased by a leading museum. If that cannot be accomplished, a leading collector who has already purchased many works by canonical artists is next-best. At the bottom of the list would be a first-time collector who has never before bought a work of art. There are reliable tales of art dealers simply refusing to sell paintings at all to collectors who—in the dealer's opinion—lack an adequate preexisting collection.) It's easy to see how the rise of NFTs will upend this utterly. There will be no "insiders" and "backroom dealers" in the art world deciding who is worthy of purchasing something.

The impact of this for consumers who would like to invest in art—but who are new to art collecting, or happen not to live in a physical location with a strong art community—is going to be an important leveling of things in more ways than one. Buying art can be a way to create intergenerational family wealth. It can be an important component of achieving the American dream. And NFTs can potentially open up this entirely new asset class for working families. Will we see more NFT sales like Beeple's, soaring high into eight figures? Of course. But we're also seeing many NFTs for sale by artists in the three- to four-figure range. Because of their connection to the blockchain and the other potential advantages that NFTs bring, it's very possible that these works of art will gradually appreciate alongside their more astronomically-expensive cousins. And even a little increase in value has the potential to make a meaningful long-term impact on the family that acquires them. In short, NFTs will take a mode of investing typically available only to the very wealthy and help it become something more and more people can afford.

This is also an area where it's a good bet that future innovations are going to help collectors out a lot. Peer-to-peer and the nascent work being done by online curators is showing some of the exciting things that are going to be possible in this area. We've only to wait and see.

One particularly interesting question being answered by lots of smart and creative people right now is: "Once you've bought an NFT, what's the *best* way to show it off?"

Just as in the world of tactile art, one of the best parts of owning a piece of art can be the cultural capital of letting people know you have it. (I'll note that some prefer to collect quietly, simply letting their artwork appreciate quietly and out of sight. That's a fine model too. I'm not here to judge!) But for those who want the thrill of display to be part of the NFT-buying experience, a vast array of options are going to be developed in the years ahead. Some may be subtle. Some may be direct and garish. Some may require technical knowledge. But virtually anyone who purchases an NFT at any price point will be able to find a fun and exciting way to share their new investment.

In the next section, we'll continue to look at the positive advantages the NFT revolution will bring for everyone across the board—and also examine how, if we do things the right way, NFTs will avoid some of the pitfalls that have dogged cryptocurrency.

PART THREE

Paths Forward for the NFT

The widespread adoption of NFTs has the potential to be revolutionary across industries, and to spark change at a level not seen since the introduction of cryptocurrency and Bitcoin. The impact of NFTs also has the potential to be even more powerful because of the way NFTs can preserve cultural artefacts, data, and digital information—essentially for all time.

NFTs are also poised to be revolutionary because digital partnerships allow almost anyone—or any brand—to create one.

Anonymous crypto-artist Pak has been a leader in early innovation for the NFT.

Minting your own cryptocurrency usually requires a significant investment of time, technology, and money, and the use of a crypto exchange to facilitate the currency's launch. Yes, a whole lot of cryptocurrencies have been issued since Bitcoin. (It's been estimated by industry leaders that there were approximately four thousand cryptos as of early 2021.) However, that figure utterly pales when compared to the number of NFTs that are being created now, and will be created in the future. As brands begin to understand the benefits of selling their content as NFTs—and using NFTs to interact with, and build bridges to, their customer bases—we're going to see something close to an exponential explosion of the amount of NFTs being used across disciplines and industries. At the corporate level, there's reason to believe that NFTs may become as integral to marketing departments as social media is today. (Just as marketing departments across the country had to add a "social media rockstar" in the early 2000s, it's likely that they're going to be posting ads for "NFT rockstars" in the very near future.)

NFTs are easy to create, they're very useful, and there are going to be lots and lots of them very soon—in just about every area of our lives that involves something digital.

Yes, major works of art like *Everydays: The First 5000 Days* will enjoy special advantages as NFTs, but so will smaller and more accessible purchases. With everything moving to digital, collectibles like trading cards will make the transition to NFT very soon. Even youngsters with more modest spending power are going to be able to enjoy the excitement that comes along with knowing they alone own the unique copy of something.

Another important part of the NFT path forward will be forged by the artists themselves. How many times have creative types heard that old chestnut, "We can't afford to pay you, but it'll be great exposure." Well, with NFTs, payment and exposure *will go hand in hand*. Creative works will be unique objects when sold as an NFT, but that doesn't mean that the art itself cannot be displayed while it is in digital form. The more that a work of art is viewed, the more the chances of it going up in value. So the owner of the NFT gets to enjoy their digital asset appreciating in value, while still being able to exhibit the physical art to everyone else as they see fit. It's a two-fer!

Another benefit to artists and content creators is going to be how and when they are paid. Under the historical model, artists only receive compensation the first time that an individual work of art they've created is sold. Artists like painters will retain the right to sell reproductions of the work in most cases—like posters made from their painting—but in any future instances in which their painting is sold from one collector to another, they will earn no new money.

Enter NFTs.

With an NFT, a creator can place protocols into the blockchain itself prescribing that whenever the NFT is sold or resold, the artist is entitled to a portion of the sale. Or a press announcement. Or whatever conditions the artists might wish to assign.

NFTs will also give artists and creator the ability to sell work entirely digitally, and without an intermediary, if they so choose. If creators want, they can contract to display their NFT in a digital gallery to get more eyes on their work, but nothing stops them from selling their work directly from their own websites and keeping the percentage that might otherwise go to an art gallery or sales agent. NFTs will also take away the anonymity of art purchasing. An artist can know who purchased one of their previous works, and/or who owns it currently. Then they can use the information to follow-up with a collector when they have a new work to sell. (In a world still reeling from the aftereffects of the COVID-19 virus, the advantages of being able to buy and sell art without physically going to a gallery hardly need to be stated.)

Some critics of the ongoing NFT revolution have expressed bafflement that collectors are willing to pay hundreds of thousands of dollars for a GIF of a digital cat when it's sold as an NFT, when the same GIF could be copied and pasted online for free. This "criticism" actually emphasizes the benefits of the NFT artwork for artists. The collectors are buying the digital work of art . . . but they're not *only* buying the digital work of art. They are buying one copy *in particular.*

Imagine there are two identical-looking paintings on physical canvases. They're so identical that each single brushstroke looks the same. What's more, the canvas and paint used is identical. The only visible difference is that one of the canvases was painted by an old master three hundred years ago, and the other was painted by a master forger using antique tools and paints. The authentic painting by the master might be worth many millions of dollars, while the forgery will be worth considerably less, even though it's virtually identical. Why? Ultimately, this is because the art collector is purchasing the fact that a celebrated old master painted this work at the moment that he or she did. It's not about whether the two paintings look the same. One was created by a certain person at a certain time, and the other wasn't.

Next, let's look at one of the most important junctures in the path ahead for the NFT. Metaphorically speaking, it's just up the road. We'll have to decide which way to go very soon. And when we make that decision, it will have large ramifications for the blockchain itself.

Proof of work versus proof of stake

One of the most important choices for NFTs will be whether they choose to rely on blockchains that utilize a Proof of Work model, or a Proof of Stake model. Don't worry if these terms are new to you; we'll explain them now.

Proof of Work and Proof of Stake are different kinds of blockchain technology. They both allow a transaction along the blockchain to be verified without the assistance of a third party. However, although they both end up at the same place, they "get there" in very different ways.

Both models are based upon cryptography. They verify transactions and ensure that every item in the blockchain maintains its integrity. To do this, Proof of Work uses unique mathematical equations that must be solved by computers. With a widespread crypto like Bitcoin—which uses the Proof of Work model—this requires a vast array of computers all around the world to be working at all times to track transactions. As noted earlier, the miners are periodically rewarded for their mining with a coin of their own. And under this system, miners with the most powerful computers will be all but assured of reaping the majority of the benefits.

Under Proof of Stake, cryptography is still used to verify history and transactions and reward network participants. However, everyone verifying the transaction has a "stake" in what is going on. With Proof of Stake cryptos, users can choose to stake a number of the coins or cryptos they hold in order to verify transactions, and a "winner" will randomly be chosen from those who have chosen to stake coins/cryptos to validate a particular block. For some Proof of Stake networks, it's like buying raffle tickets; the more you stake, the greater chance you have of winning. And if anyone ever attempted to validate a "bad block," they would lose their stake—so it helps assure a correct outcome for the process via both a carrot and a stick.

These models also work differently when it comes to environmental output. This might be the most important difference between them.

As noted earlier, the electricity used to process Proof of Work transactions just for Bitcoin now uses as much electricity as the country of Argentina! But Proof of Stake models use *millions of times less energy.*

We know that Proof of Work blockchain technology is effective at accomplishing its central stated goal, but we also know there's a tremendous environmental cost. But what if there was another technology that was just as effective, but accomplished the same goal with a negligible environmental impact? As you'll see, this question is no longer hypothetical.

Environmental impact

While many of the most notable NFTs—like Beeple's work among them—are backed by Proof of Work platforms like Ethereum, Proof of Stake platforms are the future. I believe this is fact, and not opinion.

With Proof of Stake, verification will come from a consensus (as opposed to using supercomputers racing to solve difficult math problems). All network participants are eligible to do a Proof of Stake verification—and many can be done on a laptop.

According to models, a conservative estimate is that NFTs using a Proof of Stake blockchain—like Tezos, Flow, and Polygon—will consume about *2 million times less energy* than a comparable transaction would incur on a comparable Proof of Work blockchain.

A single NFT backed by Ethereum can use the equivalent of an average person's energy consumption over an entire month during its lifetime. In contrast, an NFT with Proof of Stake is comparable to using one nightlight for about thirty minutes.

I should make a clarifying statement at this juncture. Namely, that many of the artists currently creating NFTs may not have fully understood what the environmental impact of this new form of artwork would be. The difference between Proof of Work and Proof of Stake blockchains underpinning NFTs has not always been well-explained to the artists themselves. One group seems to say, "NFTs are bad for the environment in their current form, and we need to move to Proof of Stake." The other side says, "Actually, they're not so bad . . . and we'll get back to you on the details."

Minting a coin or creating an NFT will *always* require incurring a small amount of CO2 emissions, but with Proof of Stake networks, the process will be dramatically more eco-friendly.

Will the dominant cryptocurrencies change to keep up with this model? That's one of the big questions right now.

Ethereum currently claims that it is migrating to Proof of Stake. However, it has been making this claim since 2014. Ethereum has to do this via a "hard fork" which presents a huge challenge. All users will have to update at once. Perhaps because of this issue, Ethereum has been dragging its feet. Those of us who build systems and make art that uses blockchain need to advocate for a better way *now*.

We're certainly hoping that the Proof of Stake model can become the dominant one, and help ensure that the environmental impact of NFTs stays very minimal.

We're at an important juncture for blockchain technology. We have to decide what kind of future we want. Blockchain and NFTs can rush forward under an unsustainable model like Proof of Work. This will render growth impossible beyond a certain point, will put an incredible tax on the environment, and might eventually cause the technology to "flame out" and die. Or we can make a shift—and not even a particularly painful one—and transition to Proof of Stake models for the foreseeable future. This will allow blockchain technology to continue to grow in an environmentally-sustainable way. Sounds like a no-brainer, right? Well, as we see in so many issues today, there is knowing the right thing to do, and then there is making the break to actually do it. Those who wish to invest in blockchain for the long term will have to take a brave step and break with their cohorts and colleagues in the space.

This leads us to another aspect of the path forward for blockchain technology . . .

NFTs will need to last

One of the interesting challenges that blockchain technology will help solve is what happens to an NFT if the company that has created it goes out of business. For example, companies like OpenSea are now among the leaders in selling NFTs. But as a purely hypothetical situation, what if OpenSea were ever to go out of business? Tech companies fail all the time, and it's a reasonable scenario for a consumer to wonder about. Can you still prove that you own the NFT if the company that sold it to you doesn't exist, and/or is no longer around to provide verification?

The good news is that this problem can be—and *is* being—solved.

We're working on using InterPlanetary File Systems (or IPFSs) to ensure that anyone who buys an NFT know that their purchase still exists even if something were to happen to the company selling them. An IPFS is a peer-to-peer network that can share data and information through a digital file sharing system that connects multiple devices. It is decentralized, but still allows for file storage between peers. Any peer in the network can request content verification from any other peer.

The IPFS model will replace the current model in which a business selling NFTs might do so by renting space on Amazon's servers. If something were to happen to that business's ability to rent the space (or to Amazon itself) the ability to verify ownership of that NFT might be dicey, to say the least.

But the IPFS model is instead going about the transaction in such a way that it distributes the metadata throughout peer networks. The NFP data will be on the blockchain itself, and will essentially be able to live forever.

The added security that this will bring is going to be important as more and more consumers consider dipping their toes in the digital world. Many people hesitated to invest in cryptocurrency in the 2010s because they'd heard about the Mt. Gox fiasco in which a Bitcoin exchange based in Japan announced that approximately 850,000 Bitcoins had been stolen from user wallets. Though about 200,000 were later recovered, the majority were never found. Even for members of the public unfamiliar with the inner workings of crypto-currency—or perhaps *especially* for them—this was just another reason to steer clear of blockchain investment. There was this sense that crypto meant spending your hard-earned money to invest in a thing that might just suddenly disappear one day.

While the fallout, follow-up, and litigation resulting from the Mt. Gox debacle are still ongoing, there's no question that it created confusion and set back the adoption of crypto unnecessarily. If NFTs are going to become as pervasive as they deserve to be, and reach their full potential, consumers need to understand that purchasing an NFT is a sure thing. The technology backing the purchase is strong, and there is no chance—even under far-fetched circumstances—that the NFT itself will unexpectedly cease to exist.

By pursuing IPFS-based approaches in the NFT marketplace, we can ensure that happens and lay the groundwork for a strong and lasting future for NFTs.

In the end, however, what gives us hope is that the coming impact across industries will bring new players into the space who will demand that NFTs are created the right way. They will demand security and environmental sustainability. It's one thing when artists and crypto investors get onboard. But when businesses of all types start to use NFTs, they will exert a pull—in the right direction—the likes of which we haven't seen.

In the next section, we'll look specifically at how the rollout of NFTs across industries is likely to occur, and what it will mean for all of us.

PART FOUR

The Impact of NFTs Across Industries: What to Expect in the Years Ahead

Artist Kevin Abosch created blockchain-backed digital art back in 2018, before NFT was a term people knew.

We're in the early stages. In early 2021, we were still really at the top of the first inning. However, we can still forecast the kind of changes that are probably going to ripple out from this starting point. Businesses will learn from one another. Certain industries will notice "good tricks" that are effective with NFTs, and adopt them.

Most of all, we're going to see a very significant evolution of artwork and visual representation using NFTs. There's going to be a powerful transition from static art to dynamic art on NFTs. This will do two things: One, it will create more value over time. And two, dynamic art will create a lot of value for brands from a marketing perspective.

It is this unlocking of value that will be translated across all industries through their advertising, marketing, and direct communication with their customers. It's the rising tide that's going to lift all boats.

Now let's look at how the rise of NFTs can be harnessed by artists, businesses, and creators—and what the resulting impacts will be upon their industries.

Musical artists

Performers, musical artists, and bands are in the business of selling physical items, digital items, and experiences to their audiences.

Let's start with the physical. Those among us who are a little older can still remember records being sold in record stores. Then it was tapes. Then CDs. And though most music is now sold digitally, many artists still sell physical items like t-shirts, posters, and other "merch" to their fans. (Though there have been resurgences of vinyl in recent years, consumers now purchase music overwhelmingly through digital downloads and subscription-based streaming services.) For a few old timers, it may have been a challenge to "make the leap" to digital, but today the vast majority of music fans are now comfortable accessing their favorite musicians' work on a digital platform.

DJ and producer Steve Aoki released an 11-part NFT series that has resulted in one of the most lucrative NFT launches so far.

Musicians also sell experiences. Attending a concert is an experience. Camping out at a three-day music festival is an experience. Attending an exclusive backstage "meet and greet" is an experience. In fact, as the profits from music sales have grown ever-leaner over the past twenty years, many professional musicians now earn the bulk of their incomes from this category.

I think that NFTs have the potential to be explosively successful with musical artists because of the way they're going to integrate these three areas—physical items, digital items, and experiences.

In fact, I predict NFTs will entirely disrupt the music industry.

Here's how it might work . . .

Using NFTs to create and issue tickets, the musical artist will sell tickets directly to fans for their upcoming concerts. These concert tickets will be both "pieces of art" in that they'll be NFTs that the fans will own forever and can display proudly, but they will also function as keys to unlock further experiences between the fan and the artist. The NFT ticket will provide "proof of fandom" just like a T-shirt that you purchased at a concert proves to your friends on Monday that you went to the big show that weekend. But it will also do more . . .

After the concert, the artist can use the NFT to keep in touch with the fans. The first way of doing this would be to allow NFT-holders to listen to or download a recording of the show they attended. And once the fan takes advantage of this download, they have started a digital relationship with the artist, and that can become much deeper.

The fan's NFT can unlock special information about the band. Multiple NFTs can serve to unlock different levels of rewards or experiences. You might get early access to the next album, or early access to front-row tickets during the next tour.

If you're the musical artist, you might have special luxury items or experiences you'd like to sell. For example, the guitar you played onstage during the last tour. A luxury, immersive retreat with yourself and just a few special fans in an exotic locale. But how do you identify the ultra-mega-fans who might be willing to invest serious money in these offerings? Again, you can use the NFTs-cum-tickets. A person who has an NFT ticket from every show on your last tour might be willing and able to unlock these special ultimate experiences.

Additional benefits of this system will be that agencies that regulate the selling of physical tickets can be cut out entirely, eliminating the "middleman" and potentially cutting costs for performers and fans. NFTs can also eliminate scalping and other illegal dealing in concert tickets.

NFTs can help musical artists identify potential new fans (and even help the fans themselves notice that, hey, they're really digging this great new band they're listening to). Let's explain how this might work.

So far, we've only been looking at NFTs being acquired through monetary transactions. But what if there were *other ways* that NFTs could be acquired or unlocked? Yes, a musical artist might provide a certain kind of NFT to fans in exchange for a cash payment, but what if instead the artist gave their fans an NFT in exchange for a certain activity. For example, let's say that a consumer listens to an artist's new song 100 times on a music streaming service. After the hundredth listen, the consumer receives a notification from the artist letting them know that since they're such of a fan of the song, they've been gifted an NFT. This NFT might unlock benefits from the artist such as access to new music, an invitation to a gathering for new fans, or free tickets to an upcoming local concert. From the artist's perspective, taking this first step toward fans with a "reward"-NFT can be a great way to turn potential fans or casual fans into diehard ones! This also has implications for the fandom community itself. Everybody likes to brag about being the first to discover a great new musical artist. ("When did *you* discover them? Oh really? Can you prove it by showing me the NFT for your first hundred listens?")

In the future, music fans will go from purchasing an album, song, or concert ticket to buying ownership of a fandom. This ownership concept will bring the sense of a special club along with it. The traditional "signals" one might employ to show that you're a part of fandom will still be there, but the route may be different. For example, a teenager might still wear the newest T-shirt promoting their favorite band. But the story of obtaining that T-shirt won't be "I ordered it online" or even "I went to the concert and bought it in the merch tent." Instead, the fan will have unlocked access to the shirt through the collection of NFTs that demonstrate different levels of commitment to the band.

Luxury fashion brands

Fashion brands stand to benefit tremendously from the implementation of NFTs, especially as their industry comes to rely more and more on e-commerce. Fashion and luxury brands thrive on many of the elements that NFTs help make possible, such as exclusivity, rarity, and special invitation.

Fashion brands strive for credibility with consumers. They desire wide name recognition among consumers, yet at the same time operate through creating a culture of exclusivity. Fashion and luxury consumers want items that are trendy and well-made, but they also want things that not just anybody can get.

"Luxury" captures an attitude toward the world. It puts a primacy on quality, but is also used to express the lifestyle goals and priorities of the purchaser. Those who acquire and wear luxury fashion are telling the world that they have wealth,

Supermodel Kate Moss sold a series of NFTs featuring her depicted in a variety of poses.

and that they have access to exclusive products, but they are also broadcasting that they have certain priorities and views about the world. In this way, it may emerge that the most expensive goods/brands are not always the most coveted.

Yet what *does* remain coveted is being "in the know," "high tech," "connected to exclusivity," and "ahead in the game."

Luxury fashion brands are already working to connect their products to exclusive experiences. NFTs are going to take this and absolutely explode the possibilities surrounding it.

Here's one example of how it could be done . . .

Panerai is a luxury Swiss/Italian wristwatch brand, owned by the Richemont Group. In 2019, they announced the launch of a diving watch named for the world-champion freediver Guillaume Néry. In terms of exclusivity, the watch would be priced well into five figures, and would be offered in an extremely limited edition of just fifteen watches total. That's pretty exclusive, but Panerai wasn't done. To top it off, purchasing the watch would entitle the owner to a diving lesson with Néry himself.

So, let's think about what this means. If you know about high-end watches and you encounter someone wearing the Panerai Néry, then you know that they 1) have money, 2) are connected enough to obtain a watch issued in such a limited edition, and 3) have *been invited to* take diving lessons with one of the world's greatest living divers.

Those italics are important. Some people purchasing the watch in question might not wish to try diving personally. They might simply wish to have the mystique accompanying their purchase, or they might only like the look of the watch.

But what if watch collectors *had* to have successfully completed the experience in order to gain access to the watch?

And what if that was verified by an NFT? Consider how exclusive it would be then!

When we encounter someone with an exclusive luxury brand piece, there are many possibilities around how they obtained it. Maybe they were a regular customer at a boutique, and have been clued-in to new arrivals. Maybe they have a connection at the brand itself, or know someone who works there. Perhaps they are an important influencer, and the brand is paying *them* to wear the piece. There are many different scenarios under which the consumer obtained the item. Almost all say something generally flattering about the consumer, but we don't know precisely which one is at play.

NFTs will add a laser precision to our ability to know how someone was able to obtain a luxury item, and wearing that item will soon carry a level of bragging-rights heretofore never imagined.

Suppose an NFT was *required* in order to verify that someone has had the experience necessary to purchase a luxury good. This experience could be diving with a champion free diver, yes, but it could also be performing philanthropic work, donating money to an environmental cause, attending a special event, or passing some form of challenge or test. NFTs will give fashion and luxury brands the ability to create products that are closer to "class rings" than anything else. They will be wearable fashion items that also signal specific *verified* accomplishments. Anyone can wear a diving watch to signal that they enjoy diving, but specific NFT watches will only be issued to those who have trained with specific divers, and so on.

Creator Calvin Harris held an NFT sale with a twist—only collectors who already owned 100 NFTs were eligible to purchase his work.

Obviously, the potential for cross branding here is huge. Providers of experiences will be able to partner with fashion brands on these "proof of experience" items. The possibilities are really staggering!

NFTs can also be issued to help luxury brands keep their own promises around environmentally sustainable manufacturing and fair labor practices. As millennials increasingly show that they care about the ethical side of fashion, an NFT that can verify ethical corporate behavior is going to be central. It's no longer a secret that just about anybody can *claim* to be "eco-friendly" or "humane" or whatever you like. However, if these standards can be verified by an external entity—and that entity can confirm it with an NFT written into the product's blockchain—then the game changes once again. (This will have impacts well beyond luxury and fashion. Goods across the board will want blockchain-based verification that they have been produced fairly, equitably, and with respect for the environment.)

In addition, NFTs will help fashion luxury brands by making their connections to customers feel more real and organic. Customers will be able to say "I feel like this brand really knows me" in ways that haven't been possible before. Industry research consistently shows us that consumers want a personal relationship with high-end brands. They want service that is personalized, and products that are personalized, too. They want luxury brands to be there for them at important moments in their lives, and they also want to see the brand evolving as they themselves evolve.

Using NFTs, luxury brands will be able to create a "web" of authentic experiences that can be captured for their customers. Simply by virtue of what their customers qualify to purchase, luxury brands can "know" verifiable facts about their clients at a level not currently possible. Because it will be digital and blockchain-based, this will not require front line workers to maintain an encyclopedic knowledge of each person who walks through the door; they'll be able to pull it up as easily as they can pull up a customer's account. Whether in-store sales or online purchases, brands will be able to show their connection to their customers in ways never before seen.

Static NFTs may also represent a tremendous growth area for luxury fashion brands. They will be able to create value from original fashion art, new digital artwork, and new digital merchandise. Collectible NFTs can be released to complement physical fashion product, and the two can share branding. More importantly, these Digital Fashion Items step into the ring with absolutely no limits. Luxury fashion designers can use them to create items that would never be possible in the physical world. NFTs don't come with the same restraints you get when working with fabric or leather! Designers can do just about anything they want. NFTs can also give designers a chance to showcase items from their sketchbooks that didn't make the "final cut." And if a brand decides to go one way with a design, but an alternative design released only as a collectible static NFT becomes exponentially popular, then the brand can always pivot and look at putting that item into production in the real world.

And it doesn't just have to be also-ran designs!

NFTs can forge design partnerships where NFTs provide a secret link between the real world and the virtual one. For example, Gucci could launch a new trademark shoe. They would sell the physical shoes in their physical boutiques, and could sell Static NFT artwork of the shoe through their digital presence. Then through a partnership with online games such as Roblox, Fortnite, or Animal Crossing, Gucci could sell the in-game version of the NFT, allowing gamers to put their same Gucci shoes on their digital avatar. (Look for more about the possibilities for games in a following section.)

Fashion houses are dynamic incubators of creativity. They produce illustrations, sketches, ad campaigns, photography, fashion shows, and more. NFTs exploring and commemorating this creative world are likely to have extreme attraction for devotees of the brand. Items can be sold as Static NFTs, but also as Dynamic NFTs that reimagine the added value component for VIP rewards clubs. By owning the valuable pieces of the brand, consumers become members of an exclusive group who gain exclusive access to new merchandise drops, attend special events (in-store, in atelier, fashion shows), are provided with unique services, and more.

In a Dynamic NFT-driven future, luxury customers will be "known" by brands they enjoy. Customers will come to appreciate the personalized touch and the ability they'll be given to express their interests, accomplishments, and adventures in the clothing they wear and the brands they use.

Indeed, NFTs will become a natural commercial and marketing extension within a fashion brand's normal course of business.

Sports teams and athletes

As sports teams look for ways to connect with fans in the twenty-first century, and find new ways to monetize and grow their brands, there's every sign that NFTs are going to be the tool that takes their efforts to the next level.

NBA Top Shot is allowing the NBA to monetize NFTs that capture some of the most exciting basketball

The UFC has released NFTs featuring Conor McGregor and other stars.

59

moments of all time, and is helping fans feel a new sense of ownership and connection to the league.

NBA Top Shot is the NBA's vehicle for selling NFTs to fans. The NBA is already the second most popular and profitable sports league in the United States after the NFL, so when the league went into NFTs, some in the industry were skeptical that fans who already paid for tickets, TV packages, authentic jerseys, videos games—and everything else NBA-branded—would also go in for a unique digital representation of their favorite moments from the game.

But to put it succinctly, the naysayers have already been proved wrong. Resoundingly so.

Less than nine months since launch, NBA Top Shot already has over eight hundred thousand user accounts and has generated over half a billion dollars in new revenue.

The NFTs available on NBA Top Shot offer both quality and quantity, accessibility and exclusivity. On the one hand, "packs" of NFTs (similar to packs of physical sports trading cards) are available for as little as nine dollars. On the other, the most desirable NBA Top Shot NFTs have already sold for upwards of $200,000. (Several collectors have already amassed NBA Top Shot NFT collections valued at multiple millions of dollars.)

There are many reasons why an NFT from an NBA game can be meaningful for a fan. In some cases, fans want to purchase an NFT with an image from a game they personally attended—sort of a digital analog to saving the program. In other cases, fans want to feel a sense of ownership in one of the most important games of all time. If there's an epic shot, block, or slam dunk, it speaks to them as fans to be able to own a piece of that forever. And other NBA Top Shot customers seem to like the thrill of the unknown, investing in the low-priced packs containing several "mystery" NFTs.

NBA Top Shot is also a live laboratory where other sports teams can watch live NFT business experiments with price optimization. The NBA has an enormous—yet technically finite—amount of content, stretching back to the league's first game in 1946. How can this content best be monetized? How quickly should the game's all-time most memorable images be released? We get to watch as NBA Top Shot vacillates between issuing only a single NFT image of an iconic moment, to releasing a limited amount of NFTs of an iconic moment with each one uniquely numbered like an artist's signed print.

We're also watching NBA Top Shot learn how to brand and theme its NFTs to jive with audience interest. There is considerable experimentation now with themed packs of NFTs, such as great dunks, rookie plays, All Stars, rising stars, and so on. The NBA Top Shot website regularly offers limited editions of these themed packs, and notes how quickly they sell out in order to emphasize their scarcity.

"This is all well and good," you might say. "But what if these fans are spending money on NFTs *instead of* buying other NBA collectibles? That is to say, how do you know NBA Top Shot isn't cannibalizing other NBA properties?"

It's true that 2020 and 2021 have been difficult to chart because of the impact of COVID-19, but there *is* one big indicator that NFTs don't hurt other NBA-oriented profit lines: basketball cards. Physical basketball cards saw enormous growth in late 2020 and 2021, capped off by the sale of a single card in late February of 2021 for a record setting $4.6M! If the rise in NFT is having an effect on physical collectibles, it's in a positive, not negative, direction.

Even the NBA players themselves are getting into collecting, which further drives attention to the product. NBA players routinely post videos on their social media of them opening packs of NFTs. Sometimes they hope to get an NFT of themselves, but mostly the players seem to simply enjoy collecting, just like everyone else.

One thing that will also become more measurable when the 2021–2022 NBA season opens up is if the movement into NFTs drives a new wave of fans into the stands. Enthusiasts of blockchain technology have developed their own unique culture, and the NBA has become the first professional sports league to reach out to that culture. The NBA has taken a step toward fans of digital collectibles, and it may not be a surprise if we see new fans putting more backsides in stadium seats as a result. Those who initially sought out NBA NFTs strictly as collectibles and investment vehicles may become basketball fans.

It's also worth pointing out that NBA Top Shot's NFTs may function as a "bridge" between collecting sports NFTs and collecting *objets d'art*. Bitcoins are all unique, but they aren't collectible for their own sake. Other than its history, one Bitcoin isn't going to show something special that another Bitcoin can't. And while NFT works of art have enticing visual elements, it can be difficult to know what makes them valuable. (This can be true across all forms of art. Why is a Van Gogh worth more than the best painting by the best art student at your high school? How would you spot the difference? How would you know to invest in one and not the other?)

But great feats of skill in the NBA make understanding pricing a bit easier. Even non-experts can quickly become comfortable with the idea that certain crucial plays and images from games are the most important because of what they represent. After digital collectors get comfortable moving from cryptocurrency to digital basketball plays, they may move from NFTs that capture basketball plays to NFT works of fine art. So, in this way, all boats would be lifted yet again.

As NFTs expand, the months and years ahead will continue answering our questions about how pro sports can connect with fans. Right now, the NBA is one of the only games in town. But what will the market do when there are licensed NFTs for professional football, baseball, hockey, and so on? Will the demand for NBA NFTs decline as consumers explore other sports, or will it continue to rise? Perhaps more pressingly, will there be a reward for the NBA for "getting in first"? Looking at the history of crypto technology, and the trends that drive it, there's good reason to believe that while other sports leagues may also have success with NFTs, they're going to envy the early advantage the NBA has gained.

We've looked at an entire league, but what about solo athletes?

There are interesting innovations happening in this space as well. In late March of 2021, a Croatian tennis player named Oleksandra Oliynykova sold a space on her right arm as an NFT. While the concept of selling space on a sports uniform is not new, Oliynykova took things to the next level by selling exclusive ownership to the space on her arm tied to the blockchain. Oliynykova will give the owner of the space the right to display anything of their choosing — in the form of a temporary tattoo — as long as it does not violate rules of the tennis matches in which she plays or promote hate. Importantly, Oliynykova is an up-and-coming player, whose rankings are not in the top-most tier, but are nonetheless rising. Thus, the value of this NFT has the potential to rise astronomically as she rises in the ranks.

Now let's take this real-world example and expand into the theoretical. If one can own the NFT for a space on a player, why not several players? Why not a team? Imagine the connection to the action for "superfans" (be they wealthy individuals or corporations) if they owned the NFT for a space on the uniform of their favorite athletic team?

When NFTs correlate 1:1 to items and spaces in the real world, sports and sports entertainment stand to benefit. And again, it's not just teams.

Individual athletes—even ones who play team sports—will be empowered by the opportunities that NFTs bring.

NFL star Rob Gronkowski launched his own NFT website: GronkNFT.com.

With the rise of interest among athletes in the lifestyle space, athletes will be able to bring their creative vision applicable to the lifestyle categories to new levels. NFTs will provide athletes with a direct line of communication with their fanbases. This will change the balance of power even further in the athlete's favor. When it comes to offering access to new sneakers, performance gear, training tips, tickets to sporting events—or anything at all that the athlete wants to share—the sports players themselves are going to have more of the power when it comes to connecting with—and selling to—the fanbase.

In summary, professional sports might be the best real-world example we have of NFTs creating explosive new revenue lines while empowering brands, creators, and individuals.

And it's just getting started.

Video games

Video games are an industry where NFTs are perfectly primed to explode. All the elements are ready to make the entrance of a new technology an absolutely groundbreaking event. You've got an audience accustomed to digital products and transactions, and paying for things online. Gamers are already familiar with peer-to-peer networks and forging connections online. But as much as any of this, with games, you have a culture that strives to have a literally unique gaming experience. Avatars have gone from uniform/identical, to slightly customizable, to *completely* customizable. In many contemporary video games, it's not uncommon to be able to design a character's facial features, gender, clothing, and so on. Just about every element is unique to *that* gamer playing *that* character. But what happens when the game is completed? What's left to do when the gamer is waiting around and hoping for the sequel?

This is the beginning of how NFTs can intersect with games played digitally. The idea that a much beloved avatar—with whom the gamer has literally spent hundreds or thousands of hours—might be forever lost after the game is beaten is deeply unsatisfying. But NFTs will allow players to preserve their character and its accomplishments on the blockchain forever—or sell it to someone looking to play the game next. The same things that are preserved on an NFT related to a professional athlete—his or her game stats, unique appearance, and a GIF of their signature move—can also be captured for a video game avatar. Just as an athlete might enjoy looking over a physical trophy case, a gamer can assemble a digital trophy case. Each time they complete a game, they can create an NFT of their hero that will be preserved on the blockchain for all time—even if operating systems change, or gaming consoles move on to the "next gen."

So that's a scenario for "after the game." What about before the game has been completed? What about *during* the game? Here too, NFTs bring the capacity for a transformative experience.

In the most popular cross-platform online games—Fortnite would be a good example—players are rewarded for in-game accomplishments by receiving new items, weapons, and equipment. These things can then be used to give their character a competitive advantage in the game—better camouflage, a more powerful gun, etc.—but they can also be used to give each player's avatar a tailored appearance. These items can stay with the avatar from game to game once acquired, becoming essentially a permanent part of the experience. Yet while many of the items players so enthusiastically collect are very rare—the algorithm causing them to occur only very occasionally—they are not literally unique items. If you've got a super special outfit or weapon, it still stands to reason that someone, somewhere else in the gaming universe has precisely the same loadout.

But what if they couldn't? What if it was impossible for another player to have the same weapon, or shield, or character dance move—because yours was an NFT?

Blockchain technology will allow game companies to design completely unique items available to only one player out of the thousands and thousands who might be playing the same game. Once they are obtained by the player, they can be traded or sold (as the game allows) just like any other NFT. In massive multiplayer games, this will give the players an entirely new way to make their characters distinctive and add continuity to the gaming experience.

So far in 2021, much has been made of the selling of "digital real estate" using NFTs. In just one example, in February of

2021 a player paid about $1.5 million for multiple digital properties in a video game called Axie Infinity. Using real money to purchase virtual items in video games is not new; it's been around for as long as computers and consoles have been able to process digital transactions. But previous in-game purchases have never been so astronomical. Before NFTs, players might pay an extra $20 to upgrade their character's weapon or appearance, or $60 to unlock an "add-on" portion of gameplay (such as new lands to explore or additional quests for a character to perform). It should be noted that these previous in-game transactions have generated substantial criticism from the gaming community. For example, a game might be priced at $60, but require another $20 to unlock all character traits, and another $60 to unlock all of the quests—with these latter portions available *only* through digital in-game purchases. In these cases, the gaming community will typically argue that the list price of $60 was deceptive, and that the game simply should have been priced at $140, and had all of the content included in the initial version.

What can take in-game purchases from two figures to seven figures? The answer is: the thing being purchased. People are willing to pay for exclusivity. People are willing to pay more for something that's produced in a limited edition than they are for something that comes in unlimited amounts. People are willing to pay dues to belong to exclusive clubs, associations, and societies. Having something unique and special makes people feel good, and they'll pay top dollar to feel that way.

NFTs will change video games because the things that can be purchased will not only add to the experience of the game for the player, but they will create a singular uniqueness that everyone playing the game will be able to see and feel. Imagine purchasing a castle or spaceship or sword within a game, and knowing that you're the only player in the entire world with it or that it was previously owned by a top gamer or celebrity. Yours is a "one of one" and a rare collectible.

It's also plain that there's going to be the potential for gamers to make these new in-game purchases *as investments*. (At least in games that enable players to purchase things and also to *sell* things. . . . This is a functionality that players will soon demand.) Say I'm playing a brand new video game that just debuted. The jury's out on it and the reviews are still coming in, but I like the game so I spend 1,000 real-world dollars to buy a unique magic sword for my character. In a few months, many other gamers have followed my lead and discovered this game. It becomes massively popular, and goes from thousands of players to millions. Now the demand for my sword is exponentially higher, and I may be able to turn around and sell it for ten or more times what I paid. (Conversely, those who bet incorrectly will suffer the opposite effects. Those who purchased in-game unique items solely for the purpose of reselling them later—and not out of any genuine passion for the game—will lead to a loss.)

Some companies are already setting up shop as a hub where users can buy, sell, and trade unique in-game possessions, from clothing to real estate, in NFT form. If virtual property catches on, consumers in the future may remember the present as akin to halcyon days of a digital "Oklahoma land rush" in which vast amounts of space were available virtually to all comers for very little outlay of cash.

Video games are also a space where we're clearly going to see innovations we haven't even thought about yet. There are bound to be uses for NFTs that we haven't imagined, and which go beyond merely "NFT-izing" the weapons and costumes currently sold in video games.

One fascinating example that may give us a clue to that future is coming from a new blockchain-based game called Alien Worlds. In this game, users compete to colonize and build upon alien landscapes. They form alliances and allegiances with one another, yet may break them when the time seems right. Once land in the game is controlled, it can be mined for an in-game crypto called Trillium. When it is mined, the Trillium can be used as the players see fit—to purchase land, build alliances, purchase NFT-based items, and so forth. Importantly, the creators of Alien Worlds have not specified that the Trillium mined in the game may only be used in the game. To the contrary, they have created a blockchain-based currency that users would also be able to trade in the real world. Ingeniously, this arrangement seems to blur the line between which mining is "real" and which mining is simply "playing a game."

Another great example worth discussing comes from a game developer called AnRKey X, which is developing a video game called Battle Wave 2323. While the game has not been officially launched, the format will be battle- and weapon-themed, with players picking characters and competing against one another in combat. Weapons and outfits will be part of the game—in the form of NFTs, of course—but that's not all. Players will be able to *stake* NFTs in matches when they compete against one another. This represents a serious step forward. In most fighting games, one merely fights for bragging rights. Yet in Battle Wave 2323, players will have the ability to challenge foes and potentially win their unique and valuable NFTs.

As NFTs and gaming evolve together, there will also potentially be some tough questions that will need to be answered. First and foremost, regulators will need to answer when "gaming" becomes "gambling." If a skill-based video game allows players to lose or win NFTs worth thousands of dollars, then how is this similar to, or different from, boxers betting on themselves in a boxing match?

In the United Kingdom, legislators have already taken steps to limit elements of video games like loot boxes. With a loot box, a player opens a mysterious opaque digital box that contains a random assortment of equipment to help them in the game. Loot boxes can be earned through gameplay, but they can also be purchased. British public health experts became concerned that video game loot boxes could give children a taste for online gambling. A study by a charity called GambleAware released in early 2021 found that 5 percent of video gamers spent over $100 per month on loot boxes. Considering how popular video games are, that's a huge number of people. And the press has carried sensational stories of children who incurred extremely high charges on their parents' credit cards though loot box use.

While video game manufacturers have insisted that loot boxes do not constitute or encourage gambling—and console manufacturers like Sony and Microsoft have installed controls to limit the purchasing of loot boxes on user accounts—there remains a strong backlash against them.

A future on the horizon where NFTs worth thousands are won and lost online will probably make the kerfuffle over loot boxes look like a mild disagreement in comparison. Limitations on who can play games with NFTs may be placed. The losers may be gamers under eighteen or twenty-one, who will be limited from playing some games in the same way they're limited from stepping into a casino or betting on a sport.

On the other side of the coin, there is a tremendous amount of money that stands to be made from the video game playing audience that is not yet eighteen or twenty-one. Something tells us that the companies targeting this market are going to be clever enough to incorporate NFTs into games for youngsters somehow. It would be foolish to count out the gaming industry when it comes to finding a way to reach their target markets.

In conclusion, video games represent another sphere where NFTs are all but guaranteed an incredibly rich future. The architecture is already in place, and we have every indicator that consumers will pounce once NFT integration into games begins.

Cultural institutions and venues

Museums, orchestras, ballets, and venues of all sorts will be able to harness the power of NFTs to reverse trends of diminishing sales and waning interest. They will be able to connect and reinvigorate their "tribes" of fans, and reposition themselves for powerful and meaningful growth. By connecting with their core demographics and implementing NFTs across lines of media to reach their audiences, cultural institutions will be able to leverage their assets to connect the right audience members to the right cultural experiences.

Cultural institutions straddle two worlds because they rely on both benefactors and paying customers in order to survive. How they access and engage these two groups generally makes the difference between merely surviving or fully thriving. NFTs can play a role in reaching out to both wealthy patrons and fans.

Cultural institutions are uniquely positioned to engage with their patrons and donors because they are machines for offering unique and wonderful experiences. There are the ballets and symphonies they produce, and the paintings and sculptures they put on display. Yet they can also draw on these assets to give their supporters up close and in-person events and special access in recognition of their support.

In an NFT-driven scenario, cultural institutions can solicit donations from wealthy supporters just as they do now. But while in times past, a donation above a certain dollar amount might have garnered a special invitation to a reception or event—or the chance to purchase front row tickets to an event before anybody else—the qualifications for these rewards were sometimes nebulous or unclear. And in some cases, a patron might hesitate to make a major donation if they knew that they already had plans on the night of the grand gala that was to be the award.

Patrons of the arts will also enjoy the automatic access to institutional events that they will be able to unlock with NFTs. The NFT tied to a contribution will function as a digital key, unlocking special experiences and surprises, designed to delight the most ardent supporters.

And with an NFT digital ticketing system coupled with Verifiable Credentials, these rewards can be easily customized and personalized to suit donors in new and exciting ways. Does one donor only attend operas where baritones are featured? We can get that man a behind the scenes event with the opera company's baritones as a "thank you" for his latest generous donation.

This is also true for the general audience ticketholders who may not make large donations to an institution, but still show their support through event attendance and dollars spent at the gift shop. We can also get to know these consumers through the NFTs tied to their digital ticket purchases. Cultural institutions can use the corresponding information to reach out with offerings that may be up their alley, and can make exclusive purchases available to them—much like a luxury brand would—that verify that they have been a part of certain cultural events held at the venue.

NFTs can enable fans of a museum or concert hall to gain access to the kind of custom benefits that can make them feel special and turn them into regular customers. From early seating and early entrance to events, to access to special areas, to gifts and takeaways.

NFTs will be an exciting new way for consumers to align their love for cultural institutions with other aspects of their lives. Everyone jokes about the prevalence of "NPR tote bags" among those who give to public radio. NFTs may just give those tote bags a run for their money in the years ahead!

Charities, philanthropies, and nonprofits

Charities, philanthropies, and nonprofit institutions have many elements in common with operas, museums, and cultural institutions. Both receive substantial income from large donors, but also rely on smaller amounts of income from many individuals.

Charities need to know their donor base and forge deep ties with them. Luckily, NFTs are going to help these sorts of mission-driven nonprofits to interact with their bases at a level never before seen.

In order to serve their core missions, charities need to make their presence known. They need to present themselves as the best route for addressing the problem upon which they focus—whether it's working to cure a disease, improving the environment, or addressing a social problem. To do this, they pursue traditional advertising and awareness campaigns, and also use social media. And—just like cultural institutions—charities often host branded annual events, like "runs/walks for the cause" which can help to further raise funds while giving their supporters the chance to socialize and connect personally instead of virtually.

Charities also depend on storytelling, perhaps more so than traditional businesses. Charities need to put a human face (or sometimes an animal face) on their cause. They need to show who they are helping, and how. They need to demonstrate impact, and they must do this at a macro and micro level. They can talk about thousands of sick people cured, hungry people fed, or acres of Brazilian rainforest preserved. However, they also introduce those whose lives have been personally impacted by the organization's good works.

NFTs will help charities by providing both increased seg-
mentation and increased personalization. Charities thrive by
creating lists of donors who give at certain levels. However,
they also keep lists of donors who are engaged at certain levels, and in certain ways. Who responds to a call to action on
Facebook or Twitter? Who responds only when an entreaty
is physically mailed to their house? Who shows up for events
and gatherings? Who responds to marketing material when
it's driven by data, and who gives only when instead they see
intimate personal profiles of those who have been helped by
the charity?

With NFTs, not only will these things become increasingly
easy for nonprofits to know, but in addition, supporters of
the charities will be able to incorporate NFTs into their "personal storytelling" both digitally and at events. The potential
for cultivating new "evangelists" for the cause has never been
greater.

Donors who support a charity at a
certain level, or in a certain way, can
be rewarded with a unique NFT at-
testing to their donation of money
and/or time. These NFTs can have
a visual component, and can be used
by the supporters to display their af-
fection for the charity. Certain NFTs
can also unlock benefits such as tickets to balls, galas, and other events
that the charity may hold. Donors
who are interested in personal stories
of people helped by the charity can
have this preference tracked in NFT-
form. This will allow the charity to
make more effective solicitations of

Musicians Room Service International have partnered to raise significant funds for philanthropic organizations through the release of NFTs.

the donor in the future, and can also help the donor to stay engaged.

Over time, the use of NFTs can help a charity organization demonstrate its presence in the community, and the depth of its reach with donors at all levels. (We should hasten to add here that nonprofits dedicated to preserving the environment will want to use Proof of Stake NFTs exclusively . . . but you knew that already.) Demonstrating engagement through NFTs will bring more attention to your charity, help create opportunities for cause marketing (partnerships between nonprofit and for-profit organizations for a mutual cause), and can demonstrate in a quantifiable way that your organization is having a great impact on the cause you serve.

Virtual reality and augmented reality

Virtual reality (VR) and augmented reality (AR) have uses in art, commerce, finance, worker safety, and storytelling—and a whole lot of other places too. For the sake of clarity, we'll make them a discrete industry category here, but they have applications all over.

In case you're a bit shaky on the difference, VR is usually considered a "computer simulation" of an entirely virtual world. Think of someone putting on a headset that gives them a 360-degree view in a video game, or that puts them right in the middle of a movie unfolding on all sides. Some VR experiences are passive, and the person inside the reality just sits (or stands) back and watches. Other VR environments allow the user to interact with their virtual world. In addition to entertainment, VR has applications for training and education. Pilots can fly 100 risk-free VR missions before they ever get into an actual flight deck.

You might think of AR as a close cousin of VR. AR is a little more serious, and a little more focused on the "real world." To give an example, a worker on an oil rig might wear an AR visor in addition to his hard hat. The visor would at first glance appear to be translucent—allowing him to see the world around him—but when activated the visor could give him special AR information invisible to the naked eye. When the rig worker glanced at a pressure valve, the visor might display a large number hovering over the valve showing the pressure reading. A vat containing a dangerous chemical might flash red to the worker, warning them of the extra danger. When the worker looked at his colleagues on the rig, workers with certain skill sets and job titles might have one color hovering above them, while others might have different colors; if the worker needed to quickly find a skilled employee to help him with an issue, it would be easy for him to glance around and spot the right person, even if all the workers are wearing identical uniforms.

VR and AR are being used in so many industries that it's getting hard to keep track. But the combination of NFTs with VR and AR experiences are going to take things to a whole new level—and probably boost their usage even further!

A VR or AR experience can take the form of a Dynamic NFT. For example, a brand could reward loyal customers with an NFT containing an exclusive digital experience that changes over time that they could then access using a device such as an Oculus Rift or HTC Vive.

Or what about AR? A brand might issue an NFT to its most loyal customers inviting them to an exclusive new product premiere, but make the map to get there an AR experience. A flashing dotted line—that only those with the correct NFT could see—might stretch across the city. Following it would lead to the product launch venue where a big digital "X" marks the spot. What a remarkable way to get people excited to come to an opening, meet and greet, or first access event!

There's also reason to think that VR and AR will be an important integration with Static NFTs.

By combining technology with creativity, digital art will truly enter the future and become fully immersive. Many who work in the space have been asking "What's after animation and 3D?" The answer is: a major push blurring the boundaries of reality using VR and AR.

Purchasers of Static NFTs will not only be able to view artwork on their walls, but will also be able to immerse themselves within a transformative spatial experience contained within an NFT.

Some artists will grant the holder of their artwork with the ability to unlock additional artworks and experiences.

When creators like Beeple change the game for the digital space, we can expect to see serious artists taking second and third looks at what can be created in the digital arena. There are a finite number of Sistine Chapel ceilings that can be painted in the flesh and blood world, but everything changes when artists become comfortable working in the world of VR!

Beyond NFTs

In what other spheres is blockchain technology making an impact? Read on.

Real estate

Real estate has been quietly benefitting from blockchain technology for some time already, and it stands to continue that trend.

Real estate began as an industry built around face-to-face transactions. One thinks of personal meetings with agents, touring properties in person, and showing up in offices to sign stacks of paperwork. However, digital innovation has helped the industry grow, become more accessible, and remain more competitive. Just a generation ago, it was difficult to imagine viewing a property for sale "virtually." Now, it's difficult to imagine the home buying process without this.

With innovators like Stephane De Baets tokenizing ownership of the property we are seeing still new ways that blockchain technology and real estate can be connected. Yet even changes like the one Stephane has facilitated do not paint the entire picture of what will soon become possible in the world of real estate.

Blockchain technology will make real estate leaner, faster, and more agile. When properties are tokenized, trading those tokens will allow for new ownership scenarios. Let's say a prominent commercial property has gone into bankruptcy. It has been seized and will be sold at auction by the bank. However, instead of auctioning the entire building off to one bidder, what if the bank tokenizes the ownership into a hundred thousand tokens? Theoretically, an enterprising bidder could purchase all the tokens and own the property outright. But a more realistic—and interesting—scenario is that the building will have multiple owners. As the property is once again made available to tenants, the value of those tokens will increase. (And to help the initial auction, the bank can—if it wants to—specify that the tokens can be sold back to the bank for a certain amount of fiat currency.)

Blockchain technology can also help the real estate market by speeding up transactions, and lowering costs and fees. Handling everything from taxes, to lawyers, to listings takes time and people. But new platforms and payment methods may facilitate the construction of a new industry "norm" in which transactions are recorded on the blockchain, and "middlemen" get cut out because they're rendered unnecessary. Things like the past ownership of a property, what was paid for the property, and *when* it was paid, can all be recorded on the blockchain. And so can every issue with the property that ever arose.

This lack of middlemen coupled with the immediacy with which a property's history can be known will lead to increased liquidity. Look, the real estate market is *always* going to be influenced by external forces, and the appreciation of properties will *always* necessitate the passage of time. However, when buyers and sellers *do* decide that the time is right for a sale to happen, they can both pull the trigger much more quickly with blockchain. And when it comes to fractional ownership—with blockchain-backed tokens being traded on exchanges like cryptocurrency—then the sale of fractions of a property can be practically instantaneous.

Finally, not to get too philosophical about it, but another important benefit to the rise of blockchain technology within real estate is likely to be a powerful restoration of transparency and public trust—which has the potential to help the entire industry do better.

Perhaps no economic bubble or crash in living memory has cut so deeply as the "housing bubble" which precipitated the crash of 2008. For years—and in an environment that was largely unseen by the public and regulators—the mortgage lending industry began relaxing standards for mortgage loan applications. New industry terms like NINA and NINJA loans crept their way into the lexicon, and were used to refer to these unsound new classes of borrowers. (NINA stood for "No Income No Assets" and NINJA for "No Income No Job or Assets." Essentially, banks were now willing to provide mortgage without verifying an applicant's income, assets, or employment status.) And once these risky applicants received their loans, they were often shoehorned into mortgages that they misunderstood and would not be able to repay. The most common of these was the adjustable rate mortgage. In most cases, an adjustable rate mortgage meant that the borrower would pay a low fixed mortgage rate for the first five years of the loan. But after that, it would "adjust" up to be tied to a market rate. Most borrowers did not understand how dramatic this adjustment could be, and they felt generally confident with the idea of their mortgage payment increasing somewhat because they could generally count on their incomes going up year-over-year. Then the adjustments began to hit, and horrified homeowners realized that their mortgage payments were going to go up drastically—in some cases doubling or even tripling. And in the subsequent recession this caused, many people all across the country lost their jobs, which further limited the ability of many to make their mortgage payments.

There were certainly other important factors in the 2008 mortgage debacle. These NINA and NINJA loans were subprime, yet Wall Street trading companies purchased the risky loans, bundled and repackaged them in such a way that they appeared to be much safer than they were, and sold them to pension funds, retirement funds, governments, and other entities. Then when the loans could not be repaid, these buyers of the bundled loans were left "holding the bag" financially speaking. While, again, many bad actors were to blame in this crisis, there were ultimately home mortgages at the core of what was being sold, and the incident will forever be the "mortgage crisis." As you might imagine, the fallout for the housing industry was dreadful. The market correction that began in 2008 saw home values fall by about 30 percent. Many homeowners were left underwater, and it is debatable if the housing market ever truly recovered.

But with important information about home ownership preserved on the blockchain, the ability for a massive real estate catastrophe to slowly generate in the darkness while nobody's watching becomes almost unimaginable. The blockchain can capture every part of a real estate transaction, including who purchased the property, and what level of qualification that buyer had. With this account of record, it would not be possible to purchase a bundle of risky mortgages and believe they were truly safe investments (unless you intentionally avoided doing your research). All of that information you'd need to know about what you were buying would be there on the blockchain.

Because an NFT-driven future will be a world in which transaction information can be verified peer-to-peer, everyone will feel much safer investing in real estate.

There was considerable disagreement in 2008 and after regarding who had failed to sound the alarm. Clearly—everyone seemed to agree—*someone* had been responsible for ensuring this kind of thing didn't happen. But it seemed that nobody could quite agree on who that responsible person was.

With blockchain backing real estate, that need for centralized oversight won't be necessary. A decentralized marketplace will have trust and verification built into the system.

The potential for fraud and misrepresentation will be very small, and regulators will not be needed in the way they were back in 2008.

Buyers will know the history of properties and the transactions on that property. Sellers will know about the person seeking to purchase a property. And those trading in tokenized real estate—and all of the other blockchain derivatives that are sure to come—will find that they can transact things more quickly, with much greater safety, and without the need for government regulation.

Travel and leisure

Hotels, airlines, casinos, booking services, tour companies, rental car companies—these are but a few of the players that make up the travel and leisure industries. While some vertical integration does exist, these industries are largely made up of many separate companies and chains that must work in tandem—or occasionally through official partnerships—to be collectively successful. NFTs and blockchain-based products can help these industries overcome a number of collective hurdles, and allow them to work together to serve consumers in new ways.

Using digital blockchain technology, travel and leisure providers will be able to connect more directly with customers, and use NFTs to create relationships with those customers. This will help eliminate the stranglehold that massive booking sites—like Expedia, Priceline, and Hotels.com—have over the industry.

When consumers begin to feel comfortable dealing directly with airlines, hotels, car rental companies, and adventure/experience companies, then they won't need to rely on booking sites. And when these individual travel industry providers are able to offer customized deals to their customers—often through NFTs—then consumers won't feel like they need to make a purchase through a site where these providers are pitted against one another in order to feel they are getting a good deal.

Another great advantage for consumers will come from building a peer-to-peer environment in which recommendations in the travel industry can be confirmed as organic and genuine. As the landscape currently stands, the travel and leisure business is inundated with "advertorial" content, and recommendation/review websites that masquerade as providers of original, unbiased content, but which in fact make money by generating referrals to certain travel companies, and/or that skew their editorial recommendations in exchange for compensation. These websites often make it very difficult for consumers to tell if a review or recommendation is objective or not. This leaves consumers wary and unsure if it's possible to find *any* source to trust. But peer-to-peer communities can change this.

When things like recommendations, discounts, travel policies, and rewards are tokenized and/or connected to the blockchain, travelers can feel comfortable sharing information with one another—and the sources of deals, discounts, and recommendations can be clearly verified and even sold on the secondary market. A travel and leisure provider can even issue a discount as an NFT.

What are the circumstances of this discount? Who is eligible for it? Everything is clarified for consumers right there on the blockchain.

The flow of NFTs and tokens can also work as incentives. For example, imagine a website where consumers could go to leave feedback and recommendations for their fellow travelers. With every review written or tip given, the reviewers would receive a digital reward. It could be an NFT that would grant a discount from a hotel or airline company, or it could be a crypto issued by the review site that could then be used to make a travel-related purchase. Prospective travelers could pose questions about a locale, and those answering the questions would also receive digital rewards. This would create incentives for travel experts to regularly contribute to the site to earn digital rewards, and visitors to the site would feel that they had a trustworthy source of info with reviews provided by authentic travelers—not through secretly sponsored content. Meanwhile, the company rewarding these organic reviews will be able to obtain a level of knowledge about visitors and contributors with a degree of specificity not possible in other formats.

Another way that blockchain-based products will be able to assist the travel industry is when it comes to reward programs—specifically reward points programs. A longstanding feature of the airline industry, travelers are by now quite accustomed to earning free miles and upgrades based on their frequent flyer points. Yet, what happens when an airline goes out of business, or is purchased by a competitor? Or what happens when a consumer simply wants to use their hard earned miles for things other than flights? In too many cases, the miles/points are lost forever and never redeemed. (Or, in some cases, they become redeemable at a competitor airline which the traveler dislikes.) But what if, instead of each airline issuing its own points under whatever conditions it sees fit, the airline industry agreed to settle on a crypto, NFT, or other blockchain backed product? ("AirCoin" and "MilesCoin" seem like pretty good names!) Consumers could book flights without being concerned that their points might one day be lost. Because points were safe and redeemable forever, travelers would be inclined to fly even more than they already do, confident that the perks they'd earned would always be secure. And what if a traveler suddenly decided they preferred traveling by train or boat? They would be able to go onto an exchange and sell or barter the miles they'd earned in a peer-to-peer trading network. Again, everybody wins!

In the days ahead, travel brands will be uniquely positioned to cash in on NFTs—if and when they're willing to make the leap to a world that's underpinned by NFT technology.

Health care

Most people agree that the United States health-care system has problems. Americans spend more on health care per capita than any other nation, but study after study shows that Americans do not receive the best care or have the best health outcomes. Health-care costs and health insurance prices rise year after year, and no one seems to know what to do about it. While many Americans believe the health-care system needs a complete overhaul, virtually everyone will agree that it could be made more efficient and less confusing.

Because this is an industry about which so many people have passionate opinions, it's very exciting to know that it too can be changed by the rise of blockchain technology, and potentially improved in many ways.

The problems with the health-care industry are multifaceted, but to understand how they can be corrected through blockchain technology, we need to outline them in very general terms.

The biggest issue with health care is probably cost. "Why does our health care cost so much?" is the frequent refrain. Pressed to be more specific, consumers will usually articulate their concerns as: "Why are hospital bills so high, and why does my health insurance premium increase so astronomically year-over-year?" (Others still voice frustration with the fact that these problems seem most acute within the United States, but not in many other developed countries.) To answer this—and to see how blockchain can help—let's look at it from the perspectives of the different players involved. We'll begin with the hospitals themselves, since they're the ones that set prices.

Here's a thought experiment: Imagine you win the Mega Millions lottery or the Powerball, and suddenly come into hundreds of millions of dollars. You think your town could use a better hospital, so you decide to spend your winnings to create one. You build a fancy new hospital building, fill it full of top-of-the-line medical equipment, and populate it with skilled doctors from all the top medical schools. Then, on opening day, you open the doors of your hospital and prepare to start doing business.

What happens next? Nobody comes through the door (except for a very small number of ultra-wealthy patients who can afford to pay out of pocket).

Concerned, you turn to your hospital CFO and ask, "What's going on? Why don't we have more customers? I've built the best hospital for miles around!"

Your CFO explains the problem: Most people pay for their health care *with health insurance*—which they get through their employer, or from a government exchange. The health insurance companies determine which hospitals and doctors' offices will be covered by their insurance. They call this "being in-network."

"Say no more!" you tell your CFO.

You immediately set up a meeting with the largest health insurance company in your area. At this meeting, you showcase the high quality of the hospital you've built, and make a case for the excellent care that patients will receive there.

"Wow," replies the health insurance executive. "It looks like you've really created a top-tier hospital. If people using our insurance go to your facility for treatment, it appears they are going to be cared for extremely well."

And then, just when you think you've sealed the deal, the insurance executive leans across his or her desk and asks, "So, what are you going to do for *me*?"

"Do . . . for you?" you ask innocently. "What do you mean? Isn't it enough that I've spent all this money to build the best hospital in the area?"

Both amused and bemused at your lack of worldliness, the executive will gently explain it to you this way: "If we choose to put your hospital in our insurance network, you'll immediately get thousands of paying customers. If we choose *not* to add you to our network, you'll have to subsist on self-pay customers, government programs, and a difficult patchwork of other payment methods. In other words, you *really* want to be in our insurance network. So, what if you do something for us in exchange? Specifically, what if you give people who come to your hospital with our insurance a discount of about 50 percent, right off the top. We'll call that an 'In-Network Discount' on their bill. So if there's a heart surgery that costs $100,000 on the price list, we'd like you to only charge us $50,000."

For a tense moment, you pause and try to think through your response. To your dismay, you realize the insurance executive is correct. If your hospital is going to be viable, you'll need to forge partnerships with insurance companies. But on the other hand, what they're asking is enormous. The prices at your hospital have been carefully set to generate the income you need to keep providing good care, maintain your facilities, and to pay the salaries of your well-qualified staff. And yet this insurance company wants every single one of their insured to get 50 percent off. How can you make that economically viable?

You walk out of the meeting with the insurance executive and immediately take out your cell phone and dial your CFO.

"How did the meeting go?" the CFO asks.

"Great," you tell them. "There's just one thing—we're going to double prices."

And . . . scene.

This thought experiment is not meant to pin all the blame for America's health-care issues onto insurance companies, but it does show a common perspective of one of the major players. Because hospitals know that insurance companies will demand large discounts for their members—and because hospitals absolutely need to be inside insurance networks in order to get patients—hospitals don't have an option other than to artificially inflate prices so that they'll still be able to turn a profit after network discounts are applied. But where does this leave a person paying out of pocket? The answer is, unfortunately, in a very bad position. A wealthy person paying without insurance may simply be annoyed to learn they're being charged approximately twice the rate of an insurance company. But an uninsured person of limited means may incur medical debts that are financially ruinous, or may choose not to pursue treatment at all.

Now let's look at this complex issue from another angle—which is hopefully an angle in which NFTs will also be applicable as part of a solution.

America is a land of great political diversity. State by state, and region by region, Americans often have extreme and sometimes opposing political views. When it comes to health care, some hold that it is a scandal that the US has not yet adopted a "single payer" system found in nations like Canada and England in which the government (a.k.a. the single payer of hospital bills) picks up the tab for most health care. Under such a system, citizens could still choose private pay options if they wanted to, but government-funded care would always be available. At the other end of the spectrum, large groups of Americans also believe that single payer care would result in "socialized medicine" which would lead to poor service, poor medical outcomes, and the government exerting inappropriate control over a citizen's health-care decisions.

Though attitudes about how health-care should be funded are still shifting, by and large the current mix of attitudes continues to create an absurd landscape for hospitals and health-care providers. For example, the vast majority of Americans say that hospitals should always be compelled to save someone's life in an emergency. If someone is walking past a hospital and suddenly has a heart attack, and the hospital can save their lives, Americans say that the hospital should be compelled to treat that person—whether or not they have insurance or the ability to pay. At the same time, a majority of American have *not* agreed that these situations should simply be paid for by the government.

So the health-care industry has been told that in some situations they are required to provide treatment, and yet the US government has also made clear that—so far—it will not serve as an intermediary to ensure that hospitals are paid for what they do. American politicians have sort of thrown the ball back to the health-care providers and said, "You guys figure it out from here."

Consequently, hospitals are forced to deal with what they call a "payer mix." It's industry lingo that means there is going to be a "mix" of customer types when it comes to payment. Some patients (or their insurance companies) will pay 100 percent of their hospital bill, some will pay a portion of their hospital bills, and some will pay nothing at all. The mix is different for every hospital. Health-care providers who serve prosperous communities where people tend to have employer-provided insurance will have a mix that includes very few patients who don't pay their bills. Other hospitals that serve communities of people who tend to be uninsured, underinsured, and lower-income will have a very small amount of people in their "mix" who pay 100 percent of their bills, and many who only pay a portion, or who pay nothing at all.

Consider how this payer mix situation will *also* impact the prices hospitals are forced to set. (Imagine if you ran a hardware store where the government mandated that anyone who came through the door and wanted to buy a hammer—and be billed for it later—had to be sold the hammer. And you knew that while some customers would pay the bill for their hammers, many would not pay, or would only pay a little? How would you have to price your hammers in order to stay in business?)

Finally, we should limn one other large major issue the industry faces, and that's in-network and out-of-network access to care. Many consumers—who *have* health insurance—don't grasp the way that their health insurance company may have negotiated different coverage agreements with different providers. For example, say a town has three hospitals, but a resident's insurance company may have negotiated different relationships with each of them. If that resident seeks care at Hospital A, it may be totally covered, while care at Hospital B may be only partially covered, and Hospital C not covered at all. While consumers are usually directed to the doctors and hospitals that have the most favorable network relationships, everyone seems to know someone who has found themselves in a situation where they were referred to a specialist that was not in-network and incurred large charges. In emergency situations, a physician best-qualified to treat a patient may be called in without consideration as to whether or not that provider's fee is covered by the network. Adding to the confusion, in some cases, physicians from different provider networks can have offices located in the same hospital.

In addition to these large, macro-level, systemic problems, the health-care industry faces challenges related to their ongoing dependence on outdated technology. Infamously, hospitals often still use fax machines and rely on paper filing systems for patient medical records. In the health-care industry, small inefficiencies have the potential to impact patient care.

So, these are the issues we face. Now, how can blockchain and similar digital innovations help this important but troubled industry move in the right direction?

The first issue will involve price transparency. To put it bluntly, hospitals don't like talking about their prices. This recalcitrance has manifold reasons. There is the prickly need to accommodate the discounts demanded by insurance companies, as discussed earlier. There is a resistance to openness and competition, and often simply a resistance to the large cultural and logistical changes that would be necessary to achieve complete openness about prices. But think about it. How many industries can *you* name where there's no easy access to prices for services rendered?

Some hospitals are receptive to the idea of price transparency, but even these pioneers are often hesitant to "go first" when it comes to making the prices available. Because it's so rare, the effects on that first hospital to jump into the pool are mostly unknown, and the risks seem to outweigh any possible benefits. This situation keeps even reform-minded hospitals preserving the status quo.

But what if there were a powerful force that could compel transparency, and offer such efficiencies and benefits that consumers would all but demand it?

Blockchain may be that solution. They can usher in a new era of price transparency for hospitals by tying prices to specific aspects of the hospital experience (a major surgery, a quick check-in with a physician, a few aspirin from a nurse), and by eliminating the confusion that comes with the cost of an entire "hospital stay."

With prices listed on the blockchain, consumers will have access to exactly what the costs of medical services are, and have been over time at an institution.

When consumers get a taste of transparent pricing, it will drive demand across the industry, and also create trust between patients and health-care providers. Patients will become more educated about how the industry works. Many people don't think about why the price of health care can be high. But when consumers see the reasons behind the initial prices hospitals must set, it may spur them to support insurance industry regulation and reform, or even political action.

Most importantly, transparency may encourage certain people to be more likely to seek care, which can be potentially lifesaving.

Verifiable credentials may also help to improve patient care once the patients are inside the hospitals. Medical records are moved from facility to facility as patients move. In the best cases, this happens seamlessly, but in far too many notable cases, medical records can be incomplete. Physicians have to generate entirely new medical histories each time they see a new patient. Blockchain technology could make it easy for physicians to be certain they had a definitive, tamper-proof, and complete record of a patient's history each time they had a visit. Patients traveling abroad could travel with their medical history secured on the blockchain. This could help ensure that whatever might arise, wherever in the world they were, the local physicians would have what they needed to give treatment. A peer-to-peer network between international hospitals would also make this arrangement possible, and would require no action on the part of patients.

Addressing the many challenges facing American health care is one of the biggest projects that could be undertaken with any new technology. But with something as powerful as blockchain technology, reformers will have a powerful new weapon. We can all hope that it leads to fair and equitable pricing, and superior patient care.

Government

Perhaps one day we'll elect politicians in a transparent, blockchain supported voting system, but even before then, how do we ensure that they do what they were elected to do? (At least, most of the time . . .) How do we eliminate corruption? How do we ensure government runs effectively and efficiently?

Blockchain technology has roles to play in all of these questions. While some of the challenges of government work may always be intractable, there's good reason to think that blockchain technology can help governments of all sizes make substantial improvements along many fronts.

Probably the biggest issue facing government is corruption. More specifically, the ways in which public funds are used can be extremely vulnerable to inappropriate influence.

Look, governments *need* to spend money. They need to pave roads and build playgrounds. They need to hire workers to perform essential services. But they are supposed to do this in a way that does not reward the friends and family members of the politicians in power.

Corruption involving public funds is an issue in every country around the world—whether large or small, rich or poor. Any scalable solution that could address it in a meaningful way would literally have a positive impact for every nation on earth.

So how can blockchains help? Blockchains can help by making the public procurement process completely transparent. They can eliminate ambiguity surrounding who offered what, and when. They can also make the decision-making process of the officials more transparent, eliminating the possibility of "shady backroom deals."

For example, let's say a local government needs to hire a construction company to build a new bridge. Ten different construction companies put in bids. The elected official charged with making the final decision has ties to some of the construction companies. (Maybe one is owned by his brother, and another by one of his college friends.) How can the elected official prove that whatever company he picks was selected free from undue influence?

The answer is that the election official can initiate a blockchain backed process that facilitates third-party oversight and makes crucial components of the bids transparent and unable to be retroactively altered.

Another way that blockchain technology could make this kind of process less vulnerable to corruption would be to engage smart contracts. Let's say that the elected official has a list of "dealbreaker" requirements around the project. (Overall cost, materials to be used, timeline, number of local workers to be hired, etc.) The elected official could design a smart contract that automatically rejects any bid failing to meet these minimum requirements. But more excitingly, the smart contract could be designed to automatically *accept* any bid that *does* meet a certain set of criteria. In this way, the reasons for accepting one bid over another would be perfectly transparent. There would be no question as to *why* they were accepted, because they *had* to be accepted once offered.

To be sure, the above example does not prevent *all* avenues for corruption within the procurement process. (A corrupt official could still secretly tell his friend the threshold in the smart contract that would automatically win the contract, for example.) But it still takes a monumental step forward in eliminating the possibility of anything untoward occurring in the process. And in addition to things like procurement, this system could be expanded to any other government function where the allocation of money is troublingly opaque. The bestowing of grants and charity dollars, the funding of neighborhood infrastructure, and the disbursement of social assistance money could all occur with the central information made public on the blockchain.

The other way that this technology would make governments massively more efficient and less corrupt is when it comes to registries for companies, land, homes, and all other forms of government-tracked ownership.

All around the world, corruption occurs because it is very difficult for the press or for government watchdogs to learn who owns businesses and land.

Let's say there's a neighborhood in a particular city with great demand for gas stations. However, the local zoning laws do not permit gas stations to be built on most of the existing lots. Members of the city council have the power to change the zoning on a lot. In this scenario, a corrupt member of the city council might quietly purchase a couple of houses in this neighborhood and re-zone them for gas stations, doubling or tripling their value. Then when he left office—or, if he were particularly brazen, while still in office—he could sell the houses to a company that builds gas stations.

Frustratingly, scenarios like this occur all the time, because it is difficult to easily access information regarding who owns certain assets. But here again, help is on the way! Blockchains can create everlasting records of who owns certain properties. Any change in ownership will be recorded on the blockchain, so it'll be easy to look up who bought something, who sold it, and when. Blockchain can be used to create central registries for property and business transactions that can easily be cross-checked for local politicians and elected officials. The fact that ownership records are now being tracked will have a cascade effect, dis-incentivizing other types of crime. Using properties or businesses to pay bribes, return favors, or launder ill-gotten money will become much rarer. Would-be criminals will certainly want to think twice before keeping this kind of transaction on the blockchain.

This kind of public property record can also—in some situations—keep the government from "pushing the little guy around."

The issue of "land rights" is one about which citizens can become extremely passionate. When it comes to who owns what land, there can be a frustrating amount of ambiguity. Who has the rights to hunt or fish on land, or to access the natural resources resting on or running through it, is not always clear. But by putting this information into a central, searchable database where title registries are on the blockchain, a secure, updated, and publicly verifiable resource can be created. People can easily look up where property lines fall, and know what their rights are for their property. This will eliminate ambiguity, frustration between neighbors, illegal hunting and poaching, and more.

Nascent rumblings are already underway in certain states. In 2019, Florida created a blockchain task force to study how state, county, and municipal governments could benefit from blockchain-based recordkeeping.

Back in the day, paying your property taxes in Bitcoin seemed like it would be a radical change, or a far-distant "science fiction" future. Now we're already envisioning futures where governments will be open and freer from corruption, and where ownership will be clear and searchable. It's just one more way that blockchain technology will become a powerful agent of change and progress.

Supply chain

Businesses that work in supply chain logistics bringing products to market can also see efficiencies from incorporating blockchain technology.

There are several different definitions of "supply chain" and different ideas about who technically operates in this space. We're not here to split hairs, and we can go with a "big tent" definition, because there are so many related areas in which blockchain technology can be useful for this space.

Those in the supply chain need information. They need to know where goods are that have already been sent "down the chain." They need to be able to see up the chain. They need to know what the situation is at the retail consumer market endpoint. They need to ensure that their own movements and updates are synchronized with the market.

For these reasons, supply chain work revolves around trust. Can I trust the information I am getting about the status of the chain? Do I trust a vendor or partner enough to take their word implicitly? Should this (*could* this) trust be automated?

Up and down the blockchain, there are tools to create trust and/or verify facts for supply chain businesses. When a warehouse worker inspects goods on a pallet, he does not know if the goods inside the packaging necessarily match what is presented on the label. He also doesn't immediately know the history or "story" of that pallet. But what if the worker could scan a code on the side of the pallet and access the pallet's entire shipment history? That NFT would give instant access to the pallet's entire shipment history. It would tell the worker where it had been and when, and who was involved when it was transferred. If any "pinch points" or problem areas emerge, the data reporting it will have 100 percent integrity. Nobody will be able to fudge what happened when something fails to be delivered on time.

For particularly high-value items, shipping with blockchain technology will add security. Unique identifiers on packaging can help ensure that nothing is stolen or lost during shipment. Turning in a false manifest—or using a fake inventory list—will not be possible, because the real list will be tied to the blockchain. (There are already some real world examples of this. For example, De Beers has built a blockchain-based supply chain tracing program for its diamonds.)

This technology is also going to come in handy in situations where provenance and history are important. For example, the origin countries of fruits and vegetables can also be tracked in this manner. (Did those fruits and vegetables go through a country with polluted air? Etc.) And shippers who ship goods from (or through) countries with a high rate of illegal activity or contraband will have less to worry about when it comes to being regulated or searched by the government. That information will already be on the blockchain.

This is a technology that can have a sort of "critical mass" effect on supply chain. When enough players in the industry become accustomed to working with and using blockchains to secure the integrity of the chain of goods, then a network effect will be achieved, and that can create efficiencies felt across the board.

Security and cybersecurity

Much of security and cybersecurity hinges on two questions: "Who are you?" and "Should you be here?"

When an employee walks through the security gate at their corporate office and flashes a badge, they are wordlessly answering both of these questions. This is who I am, and I'm here today because I'm an employee (or visitor).

Likewise, when an employee types a name and password into a computer in order to access secure information, they are again answering these two questions.

Yet for all of the security guards and cybersecurity reminders from the IT department, we still have not solved the problems of physical security and cyber security. Numbers fluctuate annually, but retailers generally lose around $60 billion per year in theft. And when it comes to cybercrime, globally, thieves are estimated to steal as much as half a trillion dollars each year.

Blockchain and NFTs will be a powerful tool in the war to stop crime and help businesses improve their security.

On the physical crime and retail side, NFTs can play a role in helping guard against impersonation and identity theft. For example, ID badges can be faked, and even scannable badges with digital technology can be hacked. But what about verfiable credentials? They are unique and tied to the blockchain. Imagine a worker passing though security with a verfiable credential badge. When the security guard scans the badge, they would be doing more than making sure the photo on the front matches the person, and that swiping the badge brings up the correct name on their computer. They would also be checking the badge against the blockchain itself. It would be impossible for a criminal to fake such a badge because the blockchain would immediately know.

And what about retail theft? Incorporating blockchain verfiable credentials (potentially coupled with NFTs) into physical items would help prevent black market dealers from reselling unauthorized goods. From another perspective, resale shops and pawn shops could be doubly certain that they were not buying stolen goods. A prospective buyer could inspect a token to ask, "Does this show a record on the blockchain of being sold?" If the item has been sold legitimately, that information can be added to the blockchain. Conversely, if there's no record of the sale, a prospective buyer cannot claim to have had no knowledge that they were purchasing something illegally.

In addition, blockchain's basic technology would give all users on the chain immediate access to anything inappropriate or criminal that might be occurring. Unauthorized users could be immediately detected, and from every direction. And there would be no delay in detecting this. It wouldn't be, "We were hacked!" but rather, "We are being hacked at this very moment!"

Knowing who everyone is—and if they should be doing what they're doing—will always be at the core of safety and cybersecurity. Verifiable credentials—in some cases tied to NFTs—will help make it easier to immediately establish identity, establish what goods have been used in which transactions, and make sure that only qualified people are looking to secure online locations. There will always be questions to ask to keep businesses and information secure, but in a future of NFTs, they'll hopefully be fewer and farther between.

———

Insurance

The insurance industry is going to be able to use blockchain technology to provide faster service to customers, operate in an atmosphere of increased customer confidence, and—most importantly—prevent fraud.

Although the insurance industry is constantly innovating and improving, it is still beset by stereotypes and misunderstandings that can make it difficult for customers to feel confident. There's a popular conception/feeling that even when insurance premiums are fully up to date and coverage has been secured, that insurance companies will still find a way to "not pay" when a customer needs to use a policy. In most cases, this stems from situations in which someone has failed to pay their policy minimum, or someone has simply not understood their policy. Nonetheless, the stereotype, and the resulting mistrust, still very much exists today.

Blockchains can provide a record (for the consumer and the insurance company alike) to verify that coverage has indeed been secured. It can help insurance companies provide clear frameworks for the product they offer, and can help insured consumers understand what they are purchasing when they buy the insurance.

Insurance companies depend on the data they use to formulate insurance rates for large populations. This data needs to be accurate. Even the smallest mistakes can result in big losses. If an insurance company is looking at data on, say, the rate of vehicle accidents by drivers who live in a certain zip code, they need that information to be timely and accurate. If this regular data were stored on the blockchain, the insurance company would have a record of precisely when the relevant statistics were updated, and would always know where to look in order to find the most current information possible.

Using a blockchain can also help prevent insurance fraud. One of the ways it can do this is by verifying whether an insurance policy is current or not. In most situations today where proof of insurance is required, we're often still talking paper documents. We carry paper proof of insurance cards in our wallets to verify car insurance, and plastic cards to verify that we have health and dental insurance. But providers generally need to call or login to insurance company websites to verify that the card which corresponds to an insurance policy is still in effect. But what if instead of a physical card, we carried documents tied to a blockchain that we could bring up on our personal devices? These would immediately be able to verify things like coverage status and amount of coverage. This would prevent anyone from using an outdated document to fraudulently claim coverage.

Or what about verifying information that an applicant gives to an insurance company? Whether it's employment status, income, driving record, health status—or a similar category—these facts could all be immediately verifiable for an insurance company.

Blockchain technology will also allow insurance companies to provide better service. Property and casualty insurance claims can be processed more quickly. Insurance policies can specify that payouts will be made using blockchain backed "smart contracts"—self-executing documents in which the agreement between two parties (such as a buyer and a seller) is built into the blockchain and will automatically happen when the right conditions are met in a trackable and irreversible way.

Smart contracts could automatically issue policies when the correct conditions are met, and automatically send payments to policyholders (making payments happen much faster). They would also create great clarity for consumers, eliminating any mystery as to why a claim had (or had not) been paid.

Any innovation that can create trust and clarity in the insurance industry will be welcome. Both insurer and insured do best when they trust one another, when they have access to the same data, and when they feel comfortable that no false representations can be made. Blockchain technology will help the insurance industry to fight fraud, pay claims more quickly, and verify information accuracy. This should go a long way toward improving customer responsiveness, and creating useful business efficiencies.

———

Big tech

So, we said that this was going to be a list of how NFTs and blockchain technology will impact different institutions, fields, and businesses. However, we didn't promise you that all of these impacts were going to be positive. And when it comes to "big tech" and "big data," it's definitely the case that there's going to be a loser.

Let us note right off the bat that big tech is not going to be completely undone by NFTs, but there's reason to suspect that big tech will be "taken down a peg." In the opinion of many industry observers, it's high time that such a thing happened.

The dynamic that consumers have with technology companies should predictably change when blockchain technology and NFTs become widespread. NFTs and verifiable credentials are data backed up on the blockchain. But big tech companies like Facebook and Google and Microsoft and Apple make most of their money trading in your data. You've heard that old saying: "When you're not paying for the product, then *you* are the product." It's very true when it comes to technology. Tech companies learn everything about you (or *almost* everything), and then they sell that knowledge. Big tech knows where you go online, what you type into documents, what you purchase, what digital ads you linger on . . . It knows which shopping sites you go on late at night, putting something in your virtual basket but not actually checking out. Big tech can listen to your phone conversations, or your conversation with actual live people if your phone happens to be present. It can notice the keystrokes you are typing into a document, even if you are not online.

Using these powerful—and often unsettling—tools, big tech companies are amassing large amounts of information about their users. They then monetize this information by selling it in different ways. They can sell very targeted ad space because they already know who may be interested in a product or service. Many tech companies also bundle and sell your data to third parties. We've also seen these companies trying to slowly slide into other parts of our lives; they launch payment systems, credit card–like products, and product marketplaces—hoping to expand the number of things we will choose to do on their platforms.

When a big tech company is pitching itself to potential advertisers, it says, "When it comes to your customers, I know all the things they like. I know what they're interested in. I know what they *already* want, and I know how to put something in front of their eyes to *make* them want something new."

And, largely, this is not a bluff.

Tech companies *are* enormously skilled when it comes to learning about the things that matter to consumers, and figuring out how those desires can be potentially monetized.

But maybe they are *too* skilled . . .

The United States government seems to think so. Despite significant lobbying by the industry, the CEOs of big tech have been routinely dragged in front of congress to account for this near-monopoly on online customer data. Members of congress have accused big tech of everything from intentionally promoting misinformation to serving the interests of foreign powers to crossing a line and delving too deeply into Americans' privacy.

While these hearings are probably a good thing—and the concerns voiced by the congress members and senators are very real—there is a possibility that we are about to have a powerful new tool for taking back our data from big tech. That tool will be self-sovereign identity (SSI) backed by blockchain technology.

Musician Mike Dean collaborated with artist Shepard Fairey on NFTs with audio and visual elements.

SSI are managed in a decentralized manner. This means consumers own their own data. Anything that a consumer would like to preserve on the blockchain, can be preserved. For consumers with this interest, it will no longer take a series of obscure clicks in the "customer unfriendly" part of a tech company's website to unearth data showing "what Facebook/Google/Apple knows about me." Instead, that consumer will be able to store that information by themselves and *for* themselves using a blockchain-based system.

The rise of SSI will also weaken the grip of big tech/data by creating fewer opportunities for data to be captured. Because NFTs and SSI will empower creators and institutions to strengthen their personal relationships with customers—and to sell things directly to them—the middleman/intermediary function that big tech so often plays will be reduced.

Today, I might be part of a Facebook group for fans of my favorite musician. Because Facebook has an excellent data pool on these fans, the musician (or their record company and management) might use this Facebook group to drop announcements regarding dates on an upcoming tour, or when a new album will be available for sale.

But in an SSI- and NFT-rich world, my favorite musician is already going to have lots and lots of information about me. The musician sells me tickets directly, and each ticket is an NFT that can unlock more and more layers of access. A record of what shows I've attended, what merchandise I buy, and what songs I listen to is all captured on the blockchain—potentially as a verifiable credential. In short, the musician already knows me better than Facebook ever could (when it comes to my musical taste, at least), and the musician can communicate with me, and sell things to me, better than Facebook can.

With NFTs and SSI, the relationship between creator and consumer will shift because the consumer will own their data. Though it is correct to say that big tech currently does own large amounts of consumer data, SSI will gradually allow them to take it back. More and more, the consumer will transact directly with the brand. A one-on-one relationship will be developed in which data will be exchanged, but in a closed circle. A consumer can say to a musician they like, "I choose to give my data to you, and only you." Data is owned by the consumer in sovereign fashion, and they cannot be compelled to give it out. Rather, they will share it by choice, only when and if they want to.

Politicians will continue to argue over how much access big tech companies should have to your data. This is not an issue that is going to resolve itself quickly. But as more creators and companies begin to dip their toes into the NFT pool, cracks may begin to appear in the solid modern edifice of these data giants. Very slowly, and over time, they will begin to be somewhat disarmed.

To conclude, we should note that this change does not necessarily bode ill for businesses like Facebook. The fact that consumers will have the option to interact directly with brands will push big tech to focus on its core capabilities. It will have to find ways to compete and it will improve. It will no longer overextend itself. Competition makes everyone better, and brings better products to the consumer. It's high time big tech had some real competition. That competition is going to be enabled by blockchain technology.

Did I fail to mention your industry or business in this section? If we did, don't worry. NFTs and blockchains are still on the way whether you like it or not. It's frankly beyond my poor power to add or detract from the changes they're going to bring. Wherever technology is used in the future, this technology is going to be there.

PART FIVE

New Opportunities for Investing

People want to own NFTs, but they also want to own companies involved in NFTs. During the first months of 2021, NFTs have been given a boost via strong interest from investors. The search for "NFT stocks"—that is, stocks that will support or benefit from the coming NFT boom—have surged. Some of this is coming from disciplined investors, but a certain part of it is doubtless being generated by the sense of FOMO that has driven so much recent technology investment. The point, however, is that the interest is real—and by all indicators it is growing.

Businesses that provide services that allow shared asset ownership of NFTs—or provide new ways for investors to get involved with NFTs—have done well across the board and are experiencing remarkable spikes in stock prices. Sometimes, just a rumor of associations with NFTs is enough to garner interest. Consider that in late March of 2021, word leaked that Hall of Fame Resorts & Entertainment would simply be looking into focusing on NFTs. The company's stock nearly doubled in 24 hours!

Companies have also seen surges of interest simply because of NFT "one offs." For example, Twitter CEO Jack Dorsey famously sold an NFT of his first-ever tweet for $2.9 million. (It didn't hurt that the NFT was sold in a bidding war between other famous tech icons. An NFT of a tweet by Elon Musk similarly sold in a bidding war for $1.1 million.) Dorsey didn't profit personally from the NFT, and pledged to give all money he made from the transaction to organizations fighting poverty in Africa. However, this was more than a stunt or a way to raise money for charity. It was a signal that Twitter very much intends to be and to stay at the leading edge of digital innovation.

If you're looking to "invest in NFTs" you really have three routes; you can purchase NFTs themselves, you can invest in a business that is a part of the blockchain "backend" of NFT technology, or you can invest in an existing company — that may not even be a tech company at all — which has announced that it is going to incorporate NFTs into its products and services.

Let's examine all three routes.

Purchasing NFTs

Investing in NFTs themselves is similar to purchasing works of fine art. The opportunity for the purchaser is that the work may go up in value and be resold. (Optimally, a work of art will be resold in an auction scenario, with potential buyers bidding up the price.) Just as when you are investing in physical art, when you're investing in NFTs, it helps to know "what kind of investor you are."

First of all, do you have any personal appreciation for art? Do you get a positive feeling from knowing that you own something beautiful? Or are you strictly mercenary? Are oil paintings and digital NFT images utterly interchangeable in your mind? Determining whether you personally have an aesthetic interest in the NFT art you intend to buy is a good first step in the process.

Next, it's important to know your own risk tolerance, and what your timeline is for an investment window. Are you the kind of person who feels most comfortable with a "slow and steady" gain, that's predictable and lasts many years? Or are you okay with substantial risk—and scenarios in which you may lose money on an investment—if you also have the potential to reap large rewards quickly? There are NFTs available for sale that represent both of these extremes, and everywhere in between.

How much do you know about the performance of NFTs as art? Chances are, you don't know very much because *almost nobody* knows very much. And don't believe *anyone* who tells you that they have long term information about the performance of NFTs, because there has not yet been a long term! (The person who tells you this is either exaggerating, or else has a very different definition of "long term" than most of us.) Whatever your level of knowledge going in, you'll want to learn as much as you can—right along with everyone else. The NFT market is growing, and new communities are springing up online overnight. It can be great to join others online to discuss NFTs, but always vet the information you get with the careful eye you'd apply to anything that might impact your financial future.

It's also important to keep NFTs as a fraction of your portfolio. Even those who are spending millions on NFTs right now are not going "all in." There's a reason for that. It's not that NFTs are more or less reliable investments than artworks that live in the physical world; it's that the volatility of the art market means it should only be a fraction of what you own. (There is a very small number of people who make their full-time job art collecting and sales. But unless you're going to make buying and selling NFTs into your new 9 to 5, you will want to ensure it doesn't comprise the majority of your assets —digital or otherwise.)

You'll also want to consider how much liquidity is important to you. Traditional works of physical art are not very liquid. If you want to convert them into cash—and get anywhere near a good price—you're going to have to begin a long sales process that often involves connecting with an auction house. With NFTs, you'll have more options. You may still wish to sell your NFT through an auctioneer or broker, but many of the benefits that auction houses could bring are baked into the NFT's blockchain. A potential purchaser of your art won't need a report on the provenance. They won't wonder where and when the work of art is created. The "authenticity guarantee" that blockchain brings may mean that both buyers and sellers become more comfortable doing NFT transactions independently. (And removing the cut that auction houses would take.) No one yet knows precisely how liquid the NFT art market will be once it gets going, but it's a safe bet that NFTs will always be somewhat more liquid than traditional physical artworks.

Another thing that NFT-based art and traditional physical art both have in common is that they're made by humans. Digital art captured as an NFT makes use of computer technology, but at the end of the day there is a real live artist pressing the keys. Getting to know the artists who are making art is going to be more important than ever in today's art market. The reason is that NFTs present a situation unique in art history because we're still very close to "Year 1" for all NFTs. Virtually all artists who have made an NFT artwork are still alive. In the world of paintings or sculptures, the majority of the artists whose work is commanding the highest sale prices are no longer alive. Many of them died *centuries* ago. But somehow, NFT artists are now commanding prices up there with some of the old masters of the art world, but the difference is they're not dead (and in many cases not even old). You can follow them on Twitter and Instagram, and even get to know them personally if you like. This is a jarring change that really can't be overemphasized. (We'll try italics, though.) *There is an entirely new format for high-end collectible art and virtually every single artist working in the format is still alive.* What if you could Facebook friend Van Gogh, or email Matisse, or subscribe to Basquiat's online newsletter? With NFT-based artists, 1) you can, and 2) you absolutely *should* if you plan on becoming a serious collector of NFTs. Centuries in the future, the late 2010s and early 2020s will be remembered in the art world as the "golden age" of NFTs. Not only because this was when NFTs came on the scene, but also because this was when *all* of the original NFT artists were still alive and making art. Collectors in the far future will be deeply jealous and envious of the opportunities presented to NFT collectors today. History is full of examples of collectors who became patrons of artists—and/or personal friends of them—and this resulted in an impressive collection of many of that artists' works. We're not saying you *have* to schmooze with an artist personally, but this is a great time to educate yourself and at least consider getting to know the artists who are working in the NFT format. Chances like this come along very seldom in the history of collecting!

It is also a great time to get into NFTs-as-art because we have not yet seen what the pull of "dark matter" or "dark collectors" will be . . . simply because they haven't been established yet.

For those unfamiliar, these "dark"-terms are often used in the art world to refer to forces that exert an unseen hand on the marketplace—frequently making it seem as though the art market is behaving in irrational ways. Because it's important—and *definitely* has the potential to influence NFT pricing—let's look at a hypothetical example. Let's say there was a prolific twentieth-century visual artist named "Andy W." Let's also say Andy made thousands of paintings and prints over his lifetime, and today there are thousands of people who collect his work. Some art collectors own so much of it that they have a significant financial stake in his work. Now, let's say that a print signed by Andy of a famous actress named "Marilyn" typically sells at auction for $1 million. Let us further say that there's an upcoming auction in which several of these signed Marilyns will be offered for sale at a major auction house, but many art industry experts are pointing out that there are already a glut of Marilyns out there; they conjecture that the market may be flooded, so prices could drop. However, on the day of the auction, a very strange thing happens. Each time a Marilyn goes up for sale, there is initially a bit of enthusiastic bidding, but it kind of peters out when the price gets to about $500,000. But each time this occurs, a small group of anonymous bidders jumps in. The members of this group bid against one another, and bid the price up to around $1 million. Then one of them buys the Marilyn for that amount. And this pattern seems so occur for each of Andy's works offered at this auction. What just happened? Why would a cadre of anonymous buyers swoop in to prevent the signed Marilyns from being sold at their seemingly organic price of half a mil, by bidding up the price and paying an unnecessarily high amount themselves? A dirty secret of the art world is that the anonymous (or simply unknown) buyers were probably "straw purchasers" acting on behalf of wealthy collectors who already own lots of these signed Marilyns by Andy W. They are bidding up their price because it is in their interest to ensure that the price of these works does not dip as more are added to the marketplace. And art auctions can serve as a kind of "exchange" for works of art—at which, the value of a particular artist or type of art can be set. For example, let's say I'm a wealthy art collector

Pak is a crypto artist who has been able to sell their work while maintaining complete anonymity.

and I own 100 signed Marilyns valued at about $1 million each. If there's an art auction in which a Marilyn similar to mine is sold for only $500,000, then art valuers may decide that the market must be saturated, and the *true* value of a Marilyn is now this new amount. I just lost $50 million of wealth! But now let's imagine that I know this might occur, so I have someone attend the auction on my behalf, and if it appears the Marilyn is going to sell for less than $1 million, I have my person bid it up to that. I just spent $1million to save myself $50 million.

In this way, the traditional market can feel this eerie, strange, and illogical-seeming pull exert its force when it comes to artwork sales and pricing. Of course, collectible NFT artwork is—at the end of the day—just another form of art, which means that one day it *is* likely that we will see these dark forces at work upon it. Yet importantly, for the moment, they are not exerting a strong force (if any at all). This means that those seeking to invest in NFT works of art can probably bet that they are getting something priced at what it's actually worth—free of the pull of secret forces.

Another important consideration when collecting NFT artwork is the role of institutions. The fact that prestigious museums and cultural institutions will buy works of fine art, and/or accept them as donations, is also a key driver of the art market. Those outside the art market often underestimate the pull and power that comes from museums accepting donated works of fine art.

Here's how it works: I'm a very wealthy person, and a high-end work of art is offered for sale to me at $50 million. I wonder if I should buy it. There are risks involved. The artist could fall out of favor and the value could go down. An undiscovered trove of work by the artist could be unearthed, flooding the marketplace and drastically lowering prices. In such scenarios, I might have trouble selling the work for what I paid, and I could lose wealth. However, because museums accept art from this artist as donations, I have another route—almost an "escape valve"—that helps me to feel comfortable making the purchase. When I make a donation of a work of art to a museum or institution, I know that I can declare the value of the art on my taxes as a charitable donation. So, if, one day, I have millions of dollars in income that I'd like to not pay taxes on—a common situation for a wealthy guy like me—I can use a donation of this artwork to avoid paying those taxes (because the price of the artwork will be credited as a charitable donation against my other income). This may make me comfortable pulling the trigger on purchasing that expensive work of art.

Because of this loophole/system/exemption, the interest of fine art museums in NFTs will be paramount to NFT pricing in the years ahead. If a broad-based consensus grows that museums *will* accept donations of NFT art to their collections, then the market for NFT art overall will be boosted. The prices of NFT stand to rise generally when this *does* happen. Wise investors may want to get in now, just as this is beginning to occur.

Another important consideration when it comes to NFT art investing will be overall timing in the marketplace. Right now, we're still in the early days. Yet when the dominoes begin to fall in terms of acceptance of NFT art across the board, it's very likely that at some point we're going to reach a critical mass "boom." When this happens, familiar patterns will emerge. When the general public—and investors not normally on the leading edge of technology—begin to have the sense that a booming market is underway, a lot of people will jump on the bandwagon. This can have the effect of creating a small and artificial bump in prices across the board as investors hope to make a quick buck without really understanding the market. True NFT investors will understand and appreciate the benefits of NFT artwork, and will want to hold them over the long term as their value gradually increases. But those who jump in and create a run-up in the market generally only muddy the waters for true investors. A spike happens, and even sensible investors can come away with the impression that a boom and bust has occurred. (We see this pattern in cryptocurrency investing as well.)

So what can a smart NFT investor do? When you have the sense that an initial, artificial boom is underway, remain calm and hold on to your NFTs. This is the wrong time to buy, and the wrong time to sell. If it helps, remember what happened to the price of Bitcoin in late 2017. The sudden boom sent prices hurtling at artificial speed up to $20,000. Those who anxiously sold at this price—assuming this was the most valuable Bitcoin would ever get—and those looking for a quick profit who bought at this price, both lost in the long term! (At the time of this writing, Bitcoin hovers around $60,000.) Let the market correct, then resume collecting for the long(er) term. This is the surest way to keep your head when those around you are not acting rationally.

A final, but perhaps obvious advantage of purchasing NFTs over traditional art is you won't have to factor storage and/or maintenance and/or restoration costs into the price of your investment. Even if you live in a small studio apartment, your NFT investment holdings can be enormous. You also won't need to insure your NFTs against art thieves in the same way you'd need to insure a canvas by Picasso. The fact that your ownership is built into the blockchain makes the notion of a Pink Panther–like art thief something of a relic!

In conclusion, when it comes to collecting NFT art with an eye to growing wealth, nobody is very far "ahead in the game" because the game itself has just begun. By getting yourself educated on the fundamentals and proactively learning all that you can, you're already going to be at or near the head of the pack because *this is all happening right now.* Apply the basic fundamentals of art collecting to this new manifestation of art, and you can find yourself with a collection that may be envied for many years to come.

Investing in the businesses making NFTs possible

If you're looking for opportunities that will accompany the rise of NFTs, consider the businesses that will support and accommodate every aspect of an NFT-based transaction. In this section, we'll review some of the most important businesses providing support to this new economy.

When it comes to the nuts-and-bolts of the business model of most NFT marketplaces, most take a transactional fee. What do they do to earn that fee? They work with creators, businesses, brands, and innovators to create NFTs. In some cases they finance the engineering and the programming, and can provide the creators with creative team members to augment the process with artists and animators. (This is a little bit similar to the way an artist like Jeff Koons will augment his own creations with a workshop of helpers.) Then, when the NFT sells, the marketplace pays the artist the majority of the profit, keeping a small transactional fee for themselves.

So, at a rubber-meets-the-road level, marketplaces are helping brands and artists to build and sell their NFTs, and keeping a small percentage of the profit for themselves. But in my line of work we're also doing something else. From a slightly higher elevation—metaphorically speaking—we're trying to build a community of like-minded individuals across the creative spectrum from fashion, sports, entertainment, and human rights—and giving them new tools to express themselves. We also curate the list of brands we work with in a way that opens the door for cross-branding opportunities and new promotions. For example, the cultivated consumer might appreciate listening to the music of one artist, and at the same time discovering new clothing from another brand that we feature, and also giving back to a social issue through a nonprofit that has engaged with our space using NFTs. I believe that if we focus on building the community over the long term, the value will not be transitory in nature. We're extending content to galvanize community in the long term. (More in a moment on why this is so important.)

There's a lot of interest in getting into the business of helping brands and individual artists create digital art, digital collectibles, and tokenizing (and NFT-izing) products for customers. Some businesses are creating specializations for themselves within this space. For example, they focus on helping artists create one-off pieces that will qualify as fine art and become suitable for fine art collectors. They will also work with artists to create limited series of the same work, and then position them in the same way a painter will sell signed prints. Other digital companies are cultivating specialties in digital collectibles. These companies will focus on brand partnerships and typically connect with preexisting content companies to turn their existing properties into collectible NFTs. The collectible NFTs can take the form of cards, videos clips, or badges that function as tokens with customer benefits when interacting with the parent brand. (For example, a collectible NFT may also give the customer a 10 percent discount when presented at that company's store.)

Other NFT companies will still cultivate specialties in redemption and tokenization offers, and in embedding NFTs in products that already exist. They will help musicians release music as NFTs, and video content creators to release their videos as NFTs. The unique data that the NFTs will bring will help these content creators grow new connections with their fans, and use those connections to optimize product launches in the future.

Yet other businesses in this space are going to develop the ways to showcase NFTs after consumers have purchased them. Sure, there are a few people who buy a work of fine art, a T-shirt from last weekend's big concert, or a nifty collectible, and choose to hide it away in a secret vault in the basement. But these eccentrics are few and far between! For most consumers, much of the fun and excitement of purchasing new pieces of content will come from being able to share it with friends. Developers are going to create digital carousels to feature NFTs. They're going to find ways that NFTs can be exhibited on personal websites, and it's not a stretch to forecast that social media profiles may also begin offering ways to showcase NFTs. Other developers will help consumers curate personal digital galleries where NFTs can be displayed.

When seeking out a business in the NFT business to partner with or otherwise build a mutual relationship, the overarching rule is to look for people who understand the space, have a passion for the product, and who are in it for the long term. Whenever a new innovation like NFTs hit the market, opportunists are going to swoop in and try to take advantage of the situation for short-term gain. Frustratingly, these opportunists only want a quick buck. They *don't* truly have a passion for digital, and they *don't* have the experience in the space. So how can you be certain that you're dealing with the right kind of provider? We're not here to make specific recommendations, but we can emphasize one important word: community.

There is a deep and genuine sense of community among people working in this space. They share a passion for innovation, know the lexicon, and know where NFTs are going. Those in this community are interested in building something for the long term, something that's going to last, and something that brings important change along with it.

Anybody who merely emphasizes to your brand that some fast money can be made by jumping into NFTs is probably proposing a jump that you don't want to take.

Investing in the businesses that will incorporate NFTs

When a new technology arrives on the scene, businesses—just like consumers—will adopt that technology at different rates, and along reliable pattern lines. There are always going to be:

- Pioneers/leading-edge adopters

- Early adopters

- General adoption participants

- "Feet draggers"

Whether we're talking about typewriters or computers or cellular technology, when new innovations with general, across-the-board applications show up, businesses almost always respond in ways that have them falling into these categories.

In some cases, being at or near the leading-edge can have a tremendous business advantage for a company. In other cases, adoption of this new technology does not give a company a business edge, and may even be an expense that doesn't result in a tangible advantage—but needs to be implemented just to maintain basic competitiveness.

Pioneers are those who are frequently working in the industry developing the new technology (or a subset of that industry). These pioneers are going to have special knowledge, and will become implementers of the technology well before anyone else. Most of their work happens "behind the scenes." When new breakthroughs happen for pioneers, the general business community (and the general public) is not yet aware of what's happening.

Early adopters are those who immediately see the business advantage offered by a new technology, and incorporate it into their own business as soon as they possibly can. They represent perhaps 10 to 15 percent of those who will transition to the new technology. These adopters are the first to take the risk with the technology, but also the first to reap the rewards it offers. These folks are also usually evangelists for the tech. Others in the industry will watch these early adopters closely, and use their results as an indicator of when it's time for them to take the leap themselves.

General adoption occurs when a majority of businesses decide that a new technology is appropriate for them, and that it is safe, necessary, and reliable. When new technology comes to market, those who adopt it in this category represent the vast majority of the technology's consumers—about 70 percent. Some of the folks in this category are making this change because they want to, and others because they feel they have to, but when the market reaches this point it means the change is inevitable. This technology is going to happen.

Finally, there will always be a small percentage of **those who drag their feet** when it comes to these things. This category is not large, and is usually composed of businesses who are struggling and feel they cannot afford to implement a new technology, or else are willing to risk that their business/product/service can thrive without it. (And there are always going to be a few avowed luddites who simply choose to resist change for its own sake.) In many cases, we see a business cost to being in this category, with very little advantage.

You (the reader) and I (the author) know the competitive advantages that NFTs can bring, and we've looked at how NFTs are going to revolutionize a vast number of industries. But many investors don't have our knowledge and are still unsure. And that gives *you*, the reader, an advantage when it comes to investing in the early adopter businesses.

As noted earlier, only about 10 to 15 percent of businesses fall into this category. However, we aren't anywhere near those numbers yet. There is still plenty of opportunity to identify the businesses that will enjoy the competitive advantages of early NFT adoption. At the rate things are going, by the end of 2021, we'll be lucky if we see 2 percent of businesses adopting NFT technology in a meaningful way. There's still a lot of space to get into this game.

When you're considering making an investment in a company implementing NFTs, ask yourself if the business stands to benefit according to any of the methods outlined in this book. Will the NFTs create a more direct connection between a business (or an artist) and their customers (or fans)? Does the business have a fan base that is likely to want to collect NFTs? Will new business efficiencies be unlocked and will the blockchain add value?

We're in a continually evolving space, so look for changes and updates to occur all the time. There will almost definitely be uses for NFTs that are not yet known, even by those of us working on the leading edge. (Again, this is a good thing!) When you see an early adopter business that is proposing to use NFTs in a new or novel way, they may have genuinely hit upon an important new application for the technology. You'll have to do your own due diligence and trust your instincts.

Wherever you choose to invest, connecting with the businesses who are ahead of the curve is where you'll want to be. Those willing to leap into the NFT world with both feet are going to see a massive competitive advantage. The difference between them and the 70-ish percent of businesses that follow after during the "general adoption" phase is going to be a big one. The big gains are going to be made in the next few years.

Are there any NFT-based investments to avoid? Well, as we noted earlier, the impact of big tech and big data may be a diminishment of a monopoly on customer data, and a loss of status as "middlemen" serving as intermediaries between businesses and customers. That said, Silicon Valley is still full of some of the brightest innovators on earth. Look very carefully at the way certain technology companies react to the rise of NFTs, and how they position themselves to be a part of the NFT revolution.

Final questions: regulation

We've looked at the benefits of NFTs, and the directions NFTs need to go. We've examined how certain brands are likely to be impacted by the rise of NFTs, and also at how and where NFTs are going to create tremendous opportunities for growth.

Pioneering subway graffiti artist Futura 2000 cut his teeth making art outside the law. Now he is active in NFTs.

We'll close by examining the unsettled questions still surrounding NFTs. These are areas where we don't yet know all of the answers. However, by identifying these areas of ambiguity and making a point to keep an eye on them, we can be ready to react swiftly whenever news breaks.

Exactly how will NFTs be regulated and taxed in the decades ahead?

These questions are at the very core of what the NFT future is going to hold.

Governments and regulating bodies have been slow to categorize and regulate other digital assets, like cryptocurrency, but they are finally getting there. According to many industry watchers, it was the lethargy of government to classify and regulate (or not regulate) blockchain technology that kept it from growing faster than it did. Investors were concerned that governments might suddenly declare cryptocurrency trading illegal, just as they, the investors, had finished investing heavily in it. Investing in something totally unregulated is a wild thing to do. It's like playing a game for which there are no written rules. But as the years went by, major world governments gradually aligned around a few basic tenets. By looking at these tenets, we can make some educated predictions about what the future will hold for NFTs.

Let's start with taxation.

In the eyes of the IRS, cryptocurrency and blockchain-based assets are treated as property. The IRS uses the phrase "virtual currency" to describe crypto, but it is still treated as property. When cryptocurrency is sold, those involved in the transaction must declare any gain or loss from the sale. If you are paid in cryptocurrency by someone in exchange for performing a service, you must also declare that to the IRS. However, in the eyes of the IRS you have technically been paid *with a piece of property*. Likewise, if you receive a gift of cryptocurrency, it is considered a gift of property, not of money.

And what about regulation of crypto? Here is where the lines are a little blurrier.

Experts still disagree about whether it is more appropriate to regulate cryptocurrencies as securities or commodities. **Securities** are things like stocks and bonds. People invest in them because they can be expected to increase or decrease in value. The most common interaction with a security is a long-term investment hold. **Commodities** are physical goods like oil, hogs, or corn. Most buyers of commodities purchase the goods *before they actually exist*. The buyer purchases the commodity at a set price, and then the goods are delivered in the future. Buyers are betting that the price of their commodity will rise beyond the sale price, and then the commodities can be resold for a profit. Importantly, commodities are regarded as essentially fungible. Corn here can replace corn over there. The same with hogs and barrels of oil.

In the United States, securities are regulated by the Securities and Exchange Commission (SEC), and commodities are regulated by the Commodities Future Trading Commission (CFTC).

Blockchain-based tokens sort of straddle the line between securities and commodities.

For example, some cryptocurrencies, like Bitcoin, have a set and limited supply. Only 21 million Bitcoins will ever be mined. This gives it the property of a *finite physical thing*. There are also finite amounts of gold, silver, and platinum waiting in the earth to be mined. Gold, silver, and platinum are definitely commodities, so examined from this angle, it may seem that cryptocurrency should be viewed as a commodity as well.

But there are also cryptos like Dogecoin. Dogecoin was created so that miners will generally mine 5 billion new coins per year. *However,* that total number is not capped. At various times, the creators of Dogecoin have decided to allow extra amounts of the digital currency to be created, even though this created the specter of inflation. A central authority determining that new currency can be issued, with no hard and fast ceiling in sight? This sounds less like a commodity, and more like a security issued by a government.

There are other strange aspects to crypto that also seem to stymie regulators. Bitcoins can be broken up and sold fractionally, and now usually are. If a hardware store accepts Bitcoin as a method of payment, I can walk into that store and buy a hammer with a fraction of a Bitcoin. If I have a physical bar of gold with me, would I be able to buy that same hammer by breaking off a tiny piece of gold? Or what if I only had a $100 bill, the hammer was $10, and the store had no change? Almost certainly, the hardware store would not accept a strip torn off of my Benjamin Franklin.

And what about the fact that—by the best estimates of crypto experts—about 20 percent of all Bitcoins are *not owned by anybody* . . . because they have been irreparably lost. This includes Bitcoins held in digital wallets for which the passwords have been forgotten, or Bitcoins that were held on physical external drives that were destroyed. Is this comparable to anything? It's true that commodities are often used up—hogs and corn are eaten, oil is refined—but they are not simply lost. The Federal Reserve destroys paper money when it becomes old and worn out, but that's a very small amount. (There is between 1 and 2 trillion dollars in physical US currency in circulation at any given moment. The US only destroys a number of bills valued in the low billions each year. And when it comes to money that people just accidentally misplace—or lock in a physical safe that cannot be opened—that number is far, far less.)

But the most interesting—and probably the most controversial—aspect of the classification argument around blockchain currencies is: "What can they be used for?"

Hogs can be eaten or kept as pets. Gold can be used for industrial purposes, and is universally regarded as possessing great beauty. Even if pork fell out of favor with chefs, and gold became superseded by another precious metal as "most beautiful," there is almost no chance that their value could ever fall to absolute zero.

But what about something like Bitcoin?

Examined one way, Bitcoins have a tremendous number of uses. They can immediately enable secure transaction across great distances, they can allow users to transact in a world free from the limitations of fiat currency, and they offer unparalleled accessibility as financial instruments.

Examined another way, Bitcoins have *no use at all*. They correlate to nothing in the physical world that people are typically willing to pay for. They can't be eaten, burned, smoked, or physically admired. This has caused some skeptics to argue that Bitcoins are worth nothing at all. That the benefits of Bitcoins are just that they make it easy to move around Bitcoins.

Across human history, different entities and groups have issued their own private physical currencies. Many of these currencies are worthless today, except as historical oddities. These skeptics believe that once the aura of mystery and novelty surrounding Bitcoin has been stripped away, it will return to a value of essentially zero.

These extreme swings in assessment of future value also contribute to the difficulty of deciding how cryptocurrency ought to be regulated.

(It should be noted that not every country is thinking about these questions in the same way. In Great Britain, for example, the government has created the umbrella of "cryptoassets," and beneath that, given different cryptos different classifications based on the nature of the coin. Some are considered "electronic money" and regulated like cash. Others are classified as "security coins" because they have characteristics connecting them to financial securities. Others still, like Bitcoin, fall under the classification of "unregulated coin.")

When it comes to NFTs, their status as a blockchain-backed token means that this status will influence how they're regulated. However, that's only 50 percent of the story. The other half is that NFTs generally take the form of visual art, so we can look for them to be regulated alongside the art market.

The good news here is that many of the things that concern regulators in the art world *may not apply to NFTs*.

Those regulating and monitoring the art world are interested in preventing a very specific set of crimes. NFTs will have their histories tied to the blockchain, so forgery (and fraud and impersonation) won't be a problem. (As noted, a few artists have claimed that their copyrighted works were turned into NFTs without their permission. However, these instances are very rare, and can be quickly remedied.)

A trickier issue will be money laundering, which is increasingly the number-one priority of art market regulators. There are several ways that fine art can be used to turn "dirty money" (such as from drug dealing or other criminal enterprises) into "clean money." For example, someone with "dirty money" finds an auction house or art dealer that will accept cash with no questions asked. They buy a work of art, and then immediately turn around and sell the art for approximately the same amount. Now they have a receipt for this second art sale, and that provides a "legitimate" method for how they obtained the money. Some money launderers have used variations on this, such as buying an artwork with dirty money, and then using its value to secure a loan of clean money from a financial institution. Other versions include simply colluding with a purchaser to inflate the cost of an artwork, selling it "back and forth" and bringing more illegal money into a legal transaction each time.

Another major concern in the art world is price fixing. (We examined how NFTs will be immune to this in an earlier chapter.) Still other regulators look for art that may have been stolen or "appropriated" during wars or terrorist incursions. Art in this category may not have been sold as "art" before. The items may simply be cultural antiquities that have been looted by bandits or invading soldiers.

Even the least tech-savvy regulators are going to be able to understand that NFTs are not going to be faked. And because of their link to the blockchain, there will be significant built-in safeguards against price fixing. And NFTs certainly aren't going to be looted when soldiers go pillaging museums after a battle.

This leaves money laundering, which is probably going to be the focus for regulators when it comes to NFTs. Despite the fact that NFTs are purchased digitally, regulators are still going to be very interested in the provenance of funds. "How did you get the money that was used to purchase the NFT?" is going to be the question. Buyers of NFTs will need to be prepared to answer it.

So.

Given this complex network of concerns and ambiguities, how are NFTs likely to be classified and regulated in the years ahead?

Here's my best guess:

The decisions are unlikely to be a binary, in which it's either *entirely* this, or *entirely* that. Regulators may decide that an NFT that takes the form of a $12 digital cat is fundamentally different from an NFT that's a $69-million collage sold by Christie's.

Regulators may also decide that certain NFTs should not be treated the same. NFTs that are simply used as a certificate of authenticity correlating to a physical item are unlikely to be seen as a security. But for NFTs that are offered to investors *with the explicit promise of increasing value*—like tokenized ownership in a work of art—there's a chance regulators could absolutely find that those NFTs should be regulated like securities.

There's also a strong chance that the "marketing language" or "pitch" used to sell the NFTs to buyers will determine how they are regulated. For example, if NFTs are pitched to consumers as collectibles, and the advertising around them makes this clear, then regulators may agree that they should not be any more closely watched than the sale of physical figurines. However, if those selling NFTs do a sales pitch making the NFTs sound like speculative investments that can be bought and sold for a quick return, then regulators are going to take a very different view. Believe it or not, this kind of advertising/positioning can make a *huge* difference.

Another turning point will involve how issuers of NFTs behave *vis-à-vis* attempts to influence the market. Do the companies that are creating Static NFTs and making them available for sale simply pass along the products to buyers, taking a small percentage as they do so? Or, do they themselves stockpile their own collections of NFTs—in addition to the ones they sell—and try to influence the market as a way of driving up the prices *of their own NFT holdings*? If the latter scenario becomes common, then regulators may again decide that NFT art is functioning like a security as opposed to a collectible digital figurine or baseball card.

If NFTs *are* classified as a security, there will be serious drawbacks for creators, artists, and those in the business of selling NFTs. Those selling and buying NFTs will—in many cases—be required to register with the SEC. They will also face new limitations. The transfer of NFTs would be regulated, and so would the marketing. Commercials and print ads for NFTs would probably have to include disclosures related to their potential performance as investments. Consequences for error would also be more dire. For example, in a universe where NFTs were *not* considered securities, accidentally mislabeling, misidentifying, or inaccurately describing an NFT would simply be a mistake. At worst, a charge of "false advertising" might be leveled. But in a universe where NFTs *are* considered securities, providing *any* wrong information about an NFT would be a serious crime and a violation of securities laws. Those who ran afoul would be open to severe criminal and civil penalties.

Finally, "wild card" regulation scenario—which is less likely, but nonetheless worth bringing up—is what will happen if regulators (and other government entities) get interested in NFTs that can "unlock" discounts or tickets to special events, and decide that they constitute membership in a private club. This would be tricky because almost every US state has its own definition of what constitutes a club. Under the Civil Rights Act of 1964, clubs are allowed to exclude certain groups "accidentally" but not on purpose, and that exclusion cannot be the reason for the club. For example, a yachting club can be "accidentally" all white because all of the people with yachts who have applied to join so far have happened to be white, but the yacht club can't intentionally exclude nonwhite yachters. We know that NFTs will be used to offer special access to clubs, groups, and events. An entirely different kind of regulation—involving civil rights law—could come into play if these NFTs granting access begin to be considered "club memberships." Because of this, businesses will want to avoid regulation by making sure they use NFTs in accordance with all laws governing nondiscrimination and exclusion.

In the meantime, what should businesses and creators in the NFT space do in order to remain compliant (and to limit risk generally)? Well, if you're a creator or platform and you plan to "pitch" NFTs, *don't pitch them like securities*. If you have no other course available than to emphasize and sell NFTs that are like securities, *plan to be regulated*, and don't do anything that would break a rule if your NFTs were securities in the eyes of the law.

Also, make certain that anyone encouraging the public to buy your NFTs would not violate rules governing securities if your NFTs were considered to be securities. For example, the SEC has investigated celebrities for endorsing or advertising securities products (like stocks) on their social media accounts without disclosing their relationship to the company behind the stock. (For example, not disclosing that they are a paid endorser of the brand.) We've seen already that this includes blockchain-based products. In July of 2017, the SEC issued a "Report of Investigation" into celebrity endorsements of cryptocurrency ICOs. The SEC noted that: "Any celebrity or other individual who promotes a virtual token or coin that is a security must disclose the nature, scope, and amount of compensation received in exchange for the promotion." If you use celebrity endorsements, make sure the celebrities disclose their relationship to you. If endorsers are unpaid, but own NFTs that your company sells, make sure this is also stated.

When it comes to regulators from the world of fine art, it is likely that the two areas of focus will be 1) ensuring that persons purchasing NFTs understand precisely what they are (and aren't) buying—at least while NFTs are still "new,"and 2) ensuring that NFTs are not used to launder money. The first goal can be accomplished with simple consumer education. Artists who sell NFTs directly, and platforms that sell NFTs from multiple creators, should just have an educational page—or at least links out to one—to help art buyers who may be new to the space understand what they get with an NFT.

To prevent regulatory agencies from stepping in as a response to money laundering concerns will be trickier. However, the NFT community can by putting in place its own safeguards and industry best practices. At a very high level, these might include things like:

To the surprise of many, Paris Hilton has used her notoriety to create positive change via NFTs. Back in March 2020, she sold one of the first notable NFTs—a drawing of a kitten she'd done on her iPad—for $17,000, with all proceeds going to charity.

- Creating protocols for filing "suspicious activity reports." As an industry-wide procedure, anyone dealing with an NFT transaction that, for any reason, felt a bit "fishy" should have a way to easily report this to the authorities for further investigation.

- Doing additional due diligence whenever a purchaser has a known history of criminal activity such as art fraud.

- Flagging third party purchases of NFTs. That is, noting instances in which Person A sells an NFT to Person B, but Person C pays for it.

- Conducting regular risk assessments of fraud in the marketplace, and training employees on how to detect and prevent fraud.

Despite the inherent built-in safeguards against fraud in every NFT, regulators will still find it heartening to see self-regulation. Steps like those outlined above are not challenging or cumbersome when compared to engaging with a formal government regulatory body.

In conclusion, the final regulatory status of NFTs involves guesswork—yes—but it's educated guesswork. With just a little creativity, it can be easy to see the issues that may impact NFT regulation in the future. By preparing to navigate those issues now, everyone involved in the NFT ecosystem will be better positioned for long-term success.

Slow build, explosion, or slow fade?

Beyond regulation, the other big unknown for companies in the NFT space is how NFTs will grow from here. For example, will we see a slow and gradual adoption by the marketplace? Will we see a sudden trajectory that sends their prevalence skyrocketing? Or will they swell and then fade, possibly even receding from usage in the marketplace?

It should be clear by now that we believe NFTs have a strong and reliable place in the future of art, commerce, and marketing. Even so, let's examine all possible pathways for the future, and consider how "the rest of the story" of NFTs is likely to play out.

The first scenario is that NFTs will continue to gain slow and steady footholds across industries, and take incremental steps forward. Each new business that tries using NFTs is going to be "taking one for the team" or at least taking a risk without guarantee of a reward at the end of it. But when one industry leader demonstrates the strong business advantages of working with NFTs, it will be challenging for others in the same space to avoid the urge to jump in the pool. Investors too will gradually become comfortable with NFTs as an asset class. The advantage of provable ownership rights will be irresistible. Collectors may realize this gradually, but they *will* realize it. Artists may be uncomfortable with NFTs at first, but they will follow the trends and eventually realize that NFTs can represent an entirely new income stream. As the technology slowly expands and creating NFTs becomes easier, cheaper, and more environmentally friendly, everyone can get involved in the game. Kids may start creating NFTs *just because it's fun.* In this scenario, most people who get involved in NFTs will understand what NFTs are, what blockchain is, and pretty much everybody involved will have reasonable expectations for what we can expect from the technology.

In a second scenario, NFTs take off very quickly, and *not* everybody understands what they are doing when they go out and get involved. The atmosphere is driven by FOMO.

Businesses jump into the NFT space before they completely understand 1) how NFTs can be used, and 2) in what ways NFTs can be optimized for *their* industry. Though it might sound like a good thing for NFTs to take off quickly, problems can arise if companies feel they "have to" launch NFTs.

It might sound like a strange analogy, but historians agree that a sort of FOMO like this led to the opening stages of the First World War. Countries heard that other countries were beginning to arm for a big conflict, so *they* started arming for a conflict for fear of appearing unready. They did it just because everyone was doing it, whether or not it made any sense to! It became a self-fulfilling prophecy, with a horrible result.

If enough large brands jump into NFTs "early and often," smaller or less agile brands may feel there's something wrong with them—or that they'll appear weak or out of touch—if they don't follow this lead. And what's the result? A lot of companies with NFTs they don't know how to sell. Dynamic NFTs that aren't particularly targeted, and don't do a good job of forming connections with customers. Static NFTs that go uncollected. Problematically, this will result in NFTs looking less useful and promising than they actually are. The reason will be that businesses and brands didn't look before they leapt. They rolled out NFTs that aren't useful. Now, the NFT marketplace will be able to recover from this initial overreach. The genuinely useful and desirable NFTs will still connect with consumers. However, the "boom and bust" feeling will leave a bad taste in peoples' mouths for quite some time.

The other scenario—the worst one, but, in my opinion, also the least likely one—is that NFTs will exist in a diminished form and businesses and artists might fail to take advantage of the benefits they bring. How could this happen? Well, with Static NFTs, the art market could decide that digital art isn't as important as physical art. Art historians would deem NFTs unworthy of serious study. Or the demand could fail to maintain.

We also can't leave out the creators themselves. Static NFTs are art, and art is made by artists. Will creators continue to find NFTs a fun and engaging medium in which to work? Will they determine it's artistically satisfying in the long haul? Will a painter having his or her painting made into an NFT feel a sense of pride and pleasure (or at least the sense of a nice additional revenue going into their bank account)? The art world can be fickle. If creators decide that NFTs aren't satisfying—or that another technology to emerge is more satisfying—then it's possible they could move away from creating artworks using NFTs. Another challenge would be if the marketplace determines that—while NFTs are definitely fine art, and definitely carry tremendous digital benefits— they simply aren't worth a lot of money. We've already seen tremendous fluctuation in prices of NFTs. For example, between February of 2021 and April of 2021, the price of the average NFT went from about $4,000 to about $1,250. This could be a simple correction in the market over the short term, but it could also be a sign that the value of NFTs is not going to stay in the four figures. What if everyone decides that NFTs are an excellent and useful way of selling original art . . . but also that they deserve to be priced at about $25? Beeple's $69-million sale might go down in history as an anomaly, rather than the rule. (Note: There is no long-term market data to suggest this might be true.) Finally, NFTs could become a ghost of their current selves because of the way they are tied to specific blockchains and cryptos. In April of 2021, CNN reported that the value of Ethereum had increased more than 180 percent in 2021, while at the same time noting that Ethereum is the preferred crypto blockchain network for supporting NFT transactions. This gets a little into conspiracy theory territory, but what if NFTs were being pushed by large holder of Ethereum as a form of market manipulation? This is far-fetched and hypothetical, but the idea that the popularity of NFTs could somehow be connected to a desire to spike the value of some other aspect of the technology involved is technically a possibility.

These are three major scenarios of what the future might hold, but there are certainly others. NFTs could become integrated with a new technology that doesn't even exist yet. They could be harnessed in new ways. They could be appreciated for artistic aspects that aren't even on the radar yet.

At the end of the day, however, the road ahead looks promising. The utility that underpins NFTs is not a matter of opinion or trend. The unique ability to verify content and ownership along the blockchain still makes NFTs the most secure form of content around. No matter how many artists turn toward or away from NFTs, they will remain the form of art that is easier to collect, simplest to store, and most secure against theft. This is simply a fact.

There's no question that we will experience peaks and troughs in the "sine wave" of NFT pricing—and certainly not every NFT artist can expect an experience like Beeple's—but it is extremely unlikely that we are going to see a precipitous fall. In any new technology, there are going to be bandwagon jumpers and opportunists. Some people are going to think that NFTs for their own sake are always worthy of attention and value. But as the technology proves itself again and again, "true" NFTs prevail, and those who misunderstand the usefulness of the technology simply get out of the game.

If you ask me, the future for the NFT remains extremely bright. In just about any realistic scenario, NFTs come out ahead.

Final thoughts

One of the most exciting things about NFTs is that some of the most talented people in the world are still just hearing about them for the first time. How will NFTs be used in the decades ahead to share works of art, to create communities, and empower creators and brands? How will the world of finance and financial transactions be impacted by the rise of NFTs? How will good government become even better government?

We don't know all the answers, but if recent history is any indicator, there are a number of exciting changes headed our way that nobody's even thought of yet!

Consider that in 2010, it was news when a pizza restaurant agreed to accept ten thousand Bitcoins in exchange for two large pizzas. (Today, that would make those pizzas worth about $250 million each.) The early activity we're seeing now with NFTs might be analogous to this "greatest pizza deal of all time." *We just don't know.* But this kind of excitement and possibility is all around us now.

It is also safe. NFTs benefit from being underpinned by blockchain, which has already been reviewed, revised, and regulated in the preceding years. When investors understand that they will be acquiring something backed by blockchain, they know exactly what they are getting, and can dive in without hesitation.

We're also living in times of greatly exaggerated wealth in-equality. More and more, there is a pervasive feeling that those who are already wealthy and connected have the best access to the tools that will enable them to grow that wealth. This is a complex issue that must be approached from many angles, but there's no doubt that NFTs can exert a powerful and democratizing force on the art and investing markets. Works of art like NFTs will do away with the traditional gatekeepers that can give art provenance. Instead, that provenance will be built into the blockchain, and available for anyone to access. Art will be opened up to an entirely new class of investor, and being connected and already wealthy will not be a prerequisite.

In addition to the financial aspects, a powerful cultural change is going to come with NFTs. In the past, owning a work of art meant just that—you owned something. But with NFTs, the benefits of ownership are going to be multifaceted and dynamic. Ownership might entitle you to special things—from admissions to clubs only unlocked by NFTs, to simpler things like discounts and special offers at businesses. Your NFT may be able to interact and combine with other NFTs to form things greater than the sum of their parts. Artists will know immediately when their work sells, and for how much. Confusions about ownership, provenance, and forgeries will become a relic of "the before time." Art will now be bought and sold instantly, without the need for government regulation, or visiting a physical gallery.

Owning an NFT is special and new. It will connect millionaires and billionaires who bid on items at art auctions, with teens and tweens who think their $12 NFT cat picture is really neat. It will also be mysterious. Because NFTs can do—and *be*—so many different things, when someone tells you they own an NFT, it could mean all kinds of things.

And what else?

We don't yet know what else.

But that's the thing we get to discover together.